# Learning Outside the Lines

TWO IVY LEAGUE STUDENTS WITH
LEARNING DISABILITIES AND ADHD
GIVE YOU THE TOOLS FOR ACADEMIC SUCCESS
AND EDUCATIONAL REVOLUTION

## Jonathan Mooney
### and
## David Cole

A Fireside Book
Published by Simon & Schuster
New York   London   Toronto   Sydney

FIRESIDE
Rockefeller Center
1230 Avenue of the Americas
New York, NY 10020

Fireside and colophon are registered trademarks
of Simon & Schuster, Inc.

Designed by William P. Ruoto

Manufactured in the United States of America

13  15  17  19  20  18  16  14  12

Library of Congress Cataloging-in-Publication Data

Learning outside the lines : two Ivy League students with
learning disabilities and ADHD give you the tools for
academic success and educational revolution
      p.   cm.
      1.  Learning disabled youth—Education (Higher)—
United States.   2.  Attention-deficit-disordered youth—
Education (Higher)—United States.   3.  College student
orientation—United States.

LC4818.5.L45 2000
371.9—dc21
                                                    00-041274
            ISBN 0-684-86598-X

# Acknowledgments

STANDING ON THE SHOULDERS OF GIANTS:
THANKS FROM JONATHAN

This book, and in many respects the course of my life, would never have been possible if I hadn't been lifted up by the arms of giants and placed on their shoulders. The people who have helped me, inspired me, and believed in me are the heroes in my life, and the following thanks pale in the shadows of the heights they have achieved and will continue to climb.

The first and the tallest among my life is my family, partners with me in the birth of this book. Their lives are journeys of profound personal courage and love. My sister Michelle dedicated her time to working on my story, and her contributions raised my self-awareness and elevated Chapter 1, my story, to a new level. My sister Kelly has always been my mentor, and she dedicated her time (late into many nights) to the Introduction and Chapters 1, 3, and 10. Her spirit inspired those chapters and is traced throughout them. My brother, Bill, and my sister-in-law, Lisa, supported me intellectually and financially; without them, this project would have ended the summer after my first year at Brown.

My mother. My mother is in every part of this book. She read almost every word at least five times and gave me the courage to write honestly. Most important, starting in my childhood she gave me my voice. Without that gift, my mind would have died in the din of a maddening dyslexic silence.

My father. In the last month and a half of the writing, my father proofread every word of this manuscript twice, sometimes putting in more than eight hours of work a day. I am moved to tears by his sacrifice, empowered by his love, and overwhelmed by the beauty of our relationship. This book would not have happened without him.

Throughout this process, I was also supported by the unconditional love of my girlfriend, Becky Golden. She has the biggest heart I have seen and loves me whether I write or not. Like my family, she read every chapter as an editor and proofreader. Her hand is in every word, every idea, and her support helped give birth to this book. Thanks also to her family, Linda and Jerome Golden. Linda taught me the true power of the six degrees of separation, which led me to Dr. Edward Hallowell, the coauthor of *Driven to Distraction* and author of the Foreword to this book. I am also grateful for the week spent in August 1998 finishing the book proposal in their basement, eating their food, sleeping in their beds, and drinking their coffee.

I thank Dave's family. They hosted me many times, took me out to dinner, and believed in this project with all their heart.

I thank Ned Hallowell. Ned got a call from us in August 1998; we hadn't slept in eight days, holed up in Putney, Vermont, working on a pipe dream we called this book. Ned listened graciously as two undergraduates jacked up on coffee and Ritalin pitched some obscure idea for a book. He believed in us. I stand in awe of his ability to have faith in people and to take real personal and professional risks.

And there is Jill Kneerim, my agent. God knows what she was thinking when she invited a dyslexic undergraduate to her office and signed him as an author. In the beginning, she believed more in me than I did, and her support, humor, and dedication to socially relevant writing inspired and raised me above my personal doubt. She made a childhood dream come true, and I am forever grateful and indebted to her. Thank you, Jill!

In the end, people taking risks is what made this book possible. No one took more risk than the folks at Simon & Schuster. Trish Todd believed in this book enough to take a huge risk and buy it (go Brown alums!). I would also like to thank Anne

Bartholomew for her editorial support and for believing in this book through thick and thin. Thanks Anne! Most important, I thank my editor, Tricia Medved. We worked together as partners until the end. She taught me more about writing, collaboration, and partnership than any course in the Ivy Tower. And thanks also to Lisa Considine, surrogate editor and number one fan. She jumped on board late in the game to help us light this thing up on the marketing front. Thanks Lisa!

Despite the criticism of the institution of education in this book, it would never have been possible without Brown University, one of the most progressive universities in the country. I thank the transfer admission committee for the year '97. They took a huge risk with my admission (thanks, Dean Annie Cappuccino!). I also thank Peter Hocking, boss, reader, mentor, and friend. I thank Walter Davis, who sponsored a class that started it all, for better or worse. Finally, I thank two of my most dedicated readers: Cynthia Garcia Coll, who pored over Chapter 3, and Elizabeth Taylor, who helped me tell my story. She read every word of this book twice.

Landmark College is one of the best institutions of alternative learning. It gave us an office and room and board during the summers of '98 and '99. Thanks to Frank Sopper, reader, friend, and fellow soldier in the good fight; Linda Katz, president; and the entire staff of the admissions department.

The Harry Truman Foundation supported this and my future work. Thanks to Louis Blair, executive director; Mary Tolar; and all current and future Truman Scholars committed to public service.

And for the people who do not quite fit into any neat category: thanks to Gina Macris of the *Providence Journal* for great coverage; Helaine Schupack for her support of Eye-to-Eye and lifelong commitment to students with learning disabilities/attention deficit hyperactivity disorder (LD/ADHD); John Green for his support of Eye-to-Eye and for running one of the best LD/ADHD schools in the country; the Royce Swearer and Echoing Green Fellowship for strengthening my resolve and reminding me how important this work is; David Eliot for steering me down the road to emotional clarity; the Gateway School parents, Ellen Roseman and Dr. Sherwood; Malcolm Taub for his legal services; all the parents across the country who have written to me and supported my work; Karen Thomas of *USA Today* for a courageous article; Eric Hunt for his support when the book was just a dream; Ilise who met me when I was an intern at Simon & Schuster (reading Moesha books all day) and gave her time to help me develop the proposal; and kids who wrote to me and shared their stories. They kept me going.

Finally, I thank all my friends at Brown. David Pinkowitz, my roommate from day one, stuck with me throughout this whole process (Peace, DP). Ben Holzer, who duped us all into living on 175 William Street, is a great friend; his comments on Chapter 1 profoundly affected the writing. David Flink and David Hyman, friends, mentors, and peers, ran Eye-to-Eye at Brown. Their lives inspire me, their maturity amazes me, and their passion and commitment renew my faith in our ability to change the institutions we learn in.

I also thank the Fox Point School; principal Mary Brennan runs the school I wish I had had as a child. She took a huge risk by opening her doors to Eye-to-Eye. I thank Maureen Kenner for her compassion, her faith in the program, and for being a good teacher. Finally, I thank all the Eye-to-Eye mentors. They volunteer their time on the front lines of our fight. In the end, I am simply a bureaucrat, and they are the true heroes of the work. Thanks with all my heart and love to all Eye-to-Eye mentors, especially Clayton Rockefeller, Lisa Goldschmidt, Aimee Pickett, Kent Roberts, Rachael Bibby, Sara Hill, Sara Small, and Jeremy Flattau.

And lastly thanks to David Cole. May we grow old and sit on a porch in Vermont together and laugh about the day this book went just too damn far!

## THANKS FROM DAVID

Most especially, thank you to my family—Dad, Mom, Delia, Gram.

To Frank: teacher, mentor, and friend.

Everyone at Landmark College (Dr. Katz, G-E-O-F-F, Carol, Peg, and Diane to name a few).

Karen, for helping me get myself into it all in the first place.

Hanover High School, for giving me something interesting to write about.

And to Clark and Carolina Sopper, the two coolest kids on the planet.

For my family, with love:
Whose journey inspires me,
Gives me courage;
And whose unconditional love
Heals the wounds of the past.
—Jonathan Mooney

*For those of us (few yet in number, for the way is punishing), their kin and descendants, who begin to emerge into more flowered and rewarded use of our selves in ways denied to them;—and by our very achievement bearing witness to what was (and still is) being lost, silenced.*

Tillie Olsen, from *Silences*


Our hope for this book is that it will bear witness to what is oppressed and silenced within our schools every single day. Jonathan wrote the bulk of the book based on outlines and drafts written by both Jonathan and David. We set out as a team, hoping to raise each other, and our communities, out of silence. We also remained independent, each of us recounting his own individual victories.

Together, this book, our lives, and our friendship bear witness to what can happen when we refuse to be silenced, and when we fight this oppression with passion, commitment, and courage.

# Contents

# Foreword

Yo! Hey, you, with your hands on this book. Pleased to meet you. You made a good choice with this book here.

Give me time for a few sentences, would you please do me that favor? Just hold on, before you click the book shut.

Seeing as how you picked up this book, you probably want to know something about how to learn better or learn more or learn faster or just learn period. This book is good for all that.

If you picked up this book, you probably know someone who maybe doesn't learn so good, and maybe that someone could be you, or maybe it could be someone near and dear, like your son or daughter or husband or wife. Don't feel bad. There is special talent locked in the mind of the unusual learner. The trick is to unlock it. This book can help you do just that.

The problem is, see, that somewhere a long time ago some people in a dark and stinky place decided there was something called smart and there was something called stupid, and something called good and something called bad. Smart was kids who learned their lessons well and stupid was kids that put up a fuss or didn't learn at all. Good was kids who sat still and did what they were told to do, and bad was kids who didn't do these things. That was how we looked at kids as they started out in life.

We had smart, good kids; and we had stupid, bad kids. And this was the way the world went.

You couldn't fight it, at least not easily.

If you were stupid, you had to take your lumps, right along with the bad kids, and they almost always went together.

I knew lots of stupid kids. I was stupid too. I would forget what I said or what was asked or even where I was. I could be bad, too. I would speak when not spoken to, or speak when I had an idea I liked, or sometimes I would speak just to make trouble, because trouble was a lot more interesting than whatever else was going on.

Stupid, bad kids could elude the damage done by the educational system if they were lucky. Some of them could even get very lucky and find the right schools, the gifted teachers, the good friends and triumph in the educational system, as I did. Or they could get buried. They could have teacher after teacher who shamed them, and peer after peer who teased them, counselor after counselor who just didn't get it, until they began to agree they were shameful, good-for-nothing individuals. They could be told to buckle down, shape up, and just try harder only so many times before they began to believe that they simply did not have the goods to make it in this world.

Some unusual learners went on to make a difference in this world. Abraham Lincoln was one. Winston Churchill was another. Thomas Edison was in the ranks, and Albert Einstein too. As it turns out, some of the greatest geniuses who ever lived, some of the most productive benefactors of the human race started out stupid, and bad.

But then again, many stupid, bad kids, maybe even most, didn't fare so well. They got beaten down: beaten with sticks, beaten with words, beaten with sideways glances and rules of exclusion. The fact is, you can find many such people in prisons, many on unemployment, and many casting desperately about, looking for a way to live this life without daily failure and frustration.

One of the great unrecognized dramas of childhood has been the struggle throughout history, sometimes spectacularly successful and other times dismally unsuccessful, of the unusual learner to find his best place in life.

What has gone unrecognized for centuries is that this unusual learner is not stupid, neither is he bad. Indeed, he may be gifted. He carries within his mind the cognitive equivalents of genetic mutations, the ability to recombine elements of experience in new ways.

The unusual learner is hard to teach, which makes him a target for name-calling. Stupid and bad are just two of the many words that have stung him for centuries. Wayward, slow, deviant, incorrigible, and many other essentially moral diagnoses have obscured what we are now, finally, discovering is a medical diagnosis. It turns out these kids—and the adults they become—have a lot to offer. At last we are beginning to understand.

At last, at last. At last we are answering novelist John Irving's plea, contained in what he wrote of his years in high school: "I wish I'd known, when I was a student at Exeter, that there was a word for what made being a student so hard for me. . . . Instead, I kept quiet, or—to my closest friends—I made bad jokes about how stupid I was."

For centuries, the word stupid, combined with various intensifiers like bad, lazy, willful, or weak has been used to create a moral "diagnosis." That moral diagnosis has ruined millions of lives.

Now, thanks to neuroscience, we are starting to make the medical diagnosis. We are starting to help unusual learners tap into their unusual talents. We are starting to realize how complex learning is, how destructive the concept of stupid has been, and how glorious getting the most out of a mind can be.

Enter Mooney and Cole, two young unusual learners, authors of this book you are now holding. In this brave and brilliant book they offer not only their stories—which are inspiring, funny, and wonderful—but they also offer a road map for the then-unmapped routes they took, routes others can now follow by reading this book.

They offer a guide that you, reader, or the one near and dear to you, can use to get to where you want to go. This book lays out in concrete detail what Mooney and Cole have learned in two decades of screw-ups, misunderstandings, shaftings, and successes.

As you read and learn from this book, give thanks not only for the courage and pluck of Mooney and Cole, but also for the people who have helped them and others like them along the way for centuries; give thanks for the people who have known, intuitively, for thousands of years, that there is more to learning and achievement than simply trying harder, that there is more to reaching goals than simply buckling down, that there is more to making a difference in life than just learning to conform, and that the best, most valuable thoughts and ideas come co-mingled with the messiest and least accessible.

Edward M. Hallowell, M.D.

# A Naked Introduction

The day we turned in the final draft of this book, we were supposed to run naked in midafternoon through the main campus of Brown University. (Alas, for the sake of our egos the run had to wait for the spring. It was damn cold that February morning!) We were seniors, less than six months away from graduation. The naked run was to be the consummation of a contract between two kids who had been told they would be failures their entire lives. We made the deal for the naked run during our first semester as recent transfers to Brown (Jon from Loyola Marymount University in Los Angeles and David from Landmark College, a two-year college in Putney, Vermont). We promised each other we would do the run when the book was done.

The contract was always presumed to be a joke. We were committed to writing a book, but neither one of us really believed we would ever see it in glorious black and white. You see, we were never supposed to become Ivy League students. Jon, diagnosed with dyslexia in fourth grade, was supposed to be a soccer player; if an injury ended his career, Jon would, at best, turn to coaching. Dave, diagnosed with attention deficit hyperactivity disorder (ADHD) in second grade, was a high school dropout and drug addict and was supposed to become . . . well, a high school dropout and a drug addict.

We were supposed to be a pair of statistics, not Ivy League college students, and definitely not coauthors. But when we met in the fall of 1997 at transfer orientation, we began a friendship that would ultimately give birth to this book. In our first semester at Brown, we explored our histories and our wounds from growing up in a cruel educational system that told us at an early age we were lazy, stupid, and crazy. During this time, we came to know that we were members of the LD (learning disabled)/ADHD community, a population that faces brutal oppression in our schools. After arriving at Brown (proving all the experts wrong), we came to learn that we are not inherently defective and that our stories were not the narrative of some cognitive lepers but rather case studies in a much broader struggle that consumes all of us. Our life struggles had more to do with freeing ourselves from the institution of education than transcending our own personal weakness.

We are all immersed at a young age in a vast socializing institution of education that demands emotional and intellectual sacrifices. It is a loss the very first time we sit at a desk and are told that spelling is what it means to be smart, and sitting still, rather than having compassion for others, becomes what it means to be a "good kid." It is a loss and a crime when creativity, alternative learning skills, and an individualized education take a back seat to rote memorization, standardized testing, and the misconception that all people learn the same way. In the end, we all suffer when our report card and gold stars become a reflection of who we are, become all that we are.

But the greatest lesson of our journey is that we are not tethered to the past; we can change our lives and use our education to free ourselves. At some point (at Brown/before Brown; no one can really pin down when the change happened), we got sick of all the different ways people tried to define us and we said, "Screw it." We began a mission to define ourselves for ourselves, to empower ourselves, and to use our higher education to heal old wounds, shake off old identities, and recover the lost parts of ourselves. How did we do this? You do not have to have a Ph.D to understand our approach. We stopped allowing the institution of education to define us. We took control of our education by embracing our cognitive differences, embracing the alternative ways we learn, and not feeling ashamed of ourselves anymore.

By the end of our first semester at Brown, realizing that we were not lazy and stupid, as we had been labeled for years, and knowing that so many others, LD/ADHD or not, suffer similar oppression, we realized the value in sharing our stories. We all deserve an education that gives us that experience of mastery, freedom, and empowerment. And so we set out to do the only thing more absurd than a high school dropout and a teenage illiterate meeting together at an Ivy League university: writing a book.

At that time, the prospect of a naked run on the green was the only thing that could possibly top the absurdity of our lives. And naked or not, we are now running circles around the Ivy Tower, mocking it, embracing it, using it, learning from it, and in the end, challenging this institution as we always have.

What you have in your hands is the guide we wished we had when we began our journey. Education is one of the most beautiful and liberating things we can pursue in our lives, but too often it is approached as a restrictive, punitive, linear, and moralistic act. On our journey, there were no study guides that embraced alternative learning styles, no signposts that led to personal empowerment, and no avenues for an individualized education. We needed an unconventional approach that respected our differences and our individual goals. We were forced to create this approach for ourselves because we couldn't find it anywhere else.

With this new approach in hand, we could then go back and truly take advantage of our education, specifically our higher education. College was a better environment for us than high school. Although it does have its limitations (we'll get to those in the last chapters of the book), higher education can be a learner-centered and self-directed environment, if you choose to engage with it as such. And the university is an environment that holds personal empowerment as one of its highest values.

Unlike high school, middle school, and certainly elementary school, college is truly about self-directed development and learning—ironically much more like preschool. In this environment we are expected to explore our values and, as adults, explore ideas from multiple perspectives, ultimately developing our own values and perspectives, moving away from rote memorization and regurgitation. College is also more accommodating to and inclusive of alternative learning styles. The academic accommodations to our different learning styles in college left much to be desired, but they were far superior to the vast majority of "services" provided at public high schools across the country.

This handbook comes straight from the trenches to help you find academic success and personal empowerment, and give you the tools to revolutionize your education. The core of this book is a radical approach to the institution of education that has such a stranglehold on young minds. *Learning Outside the Lines* takes a self-directed approach to education that allows you to chart your own path, set your own goals, and define your own markers for success, as opposed to jumping through someone else's hoops. This is a tool to be used by you whether you are LD/ADHD and fighting against an oppressive pathology; a fourteen-year-old facing the halls of conformity called high school; a seventeen-year-old facing an educational future that you fear is out of your control; or a college student who is sick of running the rat race, spinning your wheels. And finally, this handbook is for you if you left school, nauseated by the shame our education deals out in droves, but are considering coming back to improve your future; or if you don't know what you want to do, but you want to change.

In the end, this book is for all of us who have faced the difficulties of a narrow-minded education system, were handed restrictive template identities, lost part of our self, and now want to change our past to chart a new life course. The goal of this book is to help you use your education as a way to transcend your past, find academic success, and rediscover the part of your self that the institution of education stole from you.

### Academic Success

This book pushes the envelope of what academic success means. Unlike every other guide to school, we deemphasize grades as the meaning of academic success. A 4.0 grade point average is not the end-all and be-all of our education. Rather, academic success means defining intellectual, personal, and social goals and using the medium of higher education to achieve whatever you want to be. However, if the honor roll is your goal, using this guide will improve your grades. Academic success may mean good grades for you, or it may mean simply passing your class. This book will allow you to achieve *your* goals for *your* education.

### Personal Empowerment

The core value of the book is that your education is a time to be empowered—to gain skills, perspectives, and experiences that will shape your future in a positive way. We explore how you can use your education as a means to redefine yourself or pursue an identity that is an honest reflection of who you are. When you do this, you free yourself from your past and from having to be what now defines you, and you open up your future—the essence of what it means to be empowered.

### Educational Revolution

Educational revolution is the ultimate outcome of pursuing an education that is about personal empowerment. Using your education to become who you want to be, to learn in a way that is appropriate for your mind, stands in direct opposition to many of the oppressive values that constitute our education. Being revolutionary with your education is not hard. All you have to do is use our handbook, learn in a way that suits your mind, and follow your heart, and you are engaging in a revolutionary process.

### The Goods

This book is not a theoretical, academic textbook that stands detached from reality or pontificates about theories of learning. Nor does it have a goal in mind for you other than your finding success as you define it. We do not impose an idealized notion of success and learning on you. Rather, the contents of this book are tools for you to use in pursuit of your goals. The biggest tools of the bunch are our study skills chapters. However, for us personal empowerment and academic success came as much from internal change as they did from sound study skills.

### STRUCTURE OF THE BOOK

Part I, "Deviant Minds," explores our personal change, presenting our life journey in two personal narratives. It concludes with Chapter 3, "Institutionalized," which looks critically at the institution of education and explores concrete ways to look inward to chart our own educational path.

In Part II, "Schooled," we get down to the tools that will enable you to find academic success. These are the "alternative" study skills—the kind that are on the blacklists of teachers. Congruent with the themes of our book, the study skills are alternatives to the types of skills that assume everyone learns the same way. They are tools for revolution. All of our study skills are meant to be individualized, bringing education to the student as the student is. Our skills are about beating a system that is oppressive and unjust. And the best part of it all is that the study skills are simply good learning. They embrace all kinds of minds and access all types of alternative learning styles. Using these tools, you will learn better, get better grades, and revolutionize your education.

In Part III, "Beyond Beating the System," we explore the ultimate goals of learning outside the lines. By beating the system, taking control of your education, and redefining yourself, we explore how to create experiences that embrace the parts of ourselves that are left unrealized by traditional education. We explore concrete ways to take back the self from the institution of education and how to find new learning environments—all in an effort to live a life that is truly less ordinary.

Our lives have been anything but a linear, logical progression, moving through socially constructed markers of development. This book represents the whole picture of our journey. Although most self-help books assume a sequential development, no one lives that way. You will find throughout this book the themes, skills, and processes that we discovered almost by accident throughout our lives, tangled up with academic success, academic failure, and a whole bunch of other things—the good, the bad, and the ugly.

If at any point you find that what you are reading is irrelevant to your life, jump around, skip sections, burn part of this book if you like. This book is *your* tool. By using it on your terms and for your own reasons you are living its fundamental premise: that this is your education, and no one else's.

So go forth on your own path.

# Part I: Deviant Minds

# 1:  Jonathan

I met Leo the Late Bloomer—a lion from a children's book—
the morning of my second day of third grade. My mother
bought Leo on my first day of third grade when, standing
in front of Pennycamp Elementary School in Manhattan
Beach, California, I turned to her and asked calmly, "Why
am I stupid? I can't read; all the other kids can read. What's
wrong with me?" I must have broken her heart standing in
front of the third-grade classroom. In just a short time, I
had gone from being an energetic joyful child to a depressed
little man.

At home, I was the glue and the joy for the tensions of a
blended family that consisted of my mother, father, half-
sisters, and half-brother. Throughout my childhood, our
house was filled with passion and always with the humor and
the spirit of people who never fit in and fought at all costs to
succeed. I grew up there, and although I would leave with my
own share of wounds, my family would eventually save my
life. They loved me, an eccentric child with red hair and cow-
boy boots. Like everyone else in my family, I had a foul mouth
and was afraid of no one.

*"Leo couldn't do anything right,"* my mother read to me the
morning after I asked her why I was stupid. *"He couldn't read.
He couldn't write."* I sat in her bed, my head in her lap, listening
to her read. It was so familiar. Throughout my entire life, she
had read to me about animals that never quite fit in: *Ferdinand
the Bull, Frederick the Mouse, Curious George,* and *Paddington
the Bear.* She continued to read, *"He couldn't draw. He was a
sloppy eater, and he never said a word. 'What's the matter with*

*Leo?' asked Leo's father. 'Nothing,' said Leo's mother. 'Leo is just
a late bloomer.' "*

Born into an Irish working-class family, my mother was
bright and very likely had undiagnosed dyslexia. Having struggled with school her whole life, she saw the similarities between my schooling and what she had gone through. In her
mind school was about conformity, discipline, and power.

*" 'Better late than never,' thought Leo's father. Every day Leo's
father watched him for signs of blooming. . . . 'Are you sure Leo's
a bloomer?' asked his father. 'Patience,' said Leo's mother. 'A
watched bloomer doesn't bloom.' "*

My dad was on the other side of the family divide. He was the
valedictorian at Holy Cross College, and after getting a master's
degree in teaching from the University of Chicago, he received a
law degree from Georgetown, where he was selected to the *Law
Review*. He loved me more than anything he had ever loved in his
life. But when I hid in the bathroom, afraid to make the morning
ride to school, or when I stumbled over words and could not
learn to spell my name, I believed he was ashamed of me. I felt as
if I needed to work harder, to be smarter for him to love me.

*"So Leo's father watched television instead of Leo. The snow
came. Leo's father wasn't watching. But Leo still wasn't blooming. The trees budded. Leo's father wasn't watching. But Leo still
wasn't blooming. Then one day, in his own good time, Leo
bloomed."*

When my mother hit this point in the story, she always
smiled, and I smiled too, but I also turned to her and said, "Leo
would have been fucked if he was ever in Mrs. C's class."

Mrs. C, a graying and slightly balding woman in her mid-
forties, was my second-grade teacher, who taught me to be
ashamed of myself. In her class, school was no longer a safe
place about playing with blocks and working with other kids,
things that I was good at. In first grade, I could not remember
the months of the year or the days of the week to save my life.
But my teacher told me that I was okay, that kids learn at their

own pace, and she let me play with blocks. Mrs. C did not believe in that. The first day of second grade I was greeted with a desk and was told that I had to sit there the entire day. There was no play time, only a twenty-minute recess. For me, every day of second grade was a series of painful tasks to endure. I couldn't tell time, I couldn't spell, and reading was the most traumatic of all.

I was in the blue jay reading circle, reading, "See Spot run," most days. I knew what kind of reading group I was in. My circle met on the right side of the classroom, all the way across the room from my desk. Gathering my books like all the other kids, we methodically moved to our different circles: the robins, the hawks, the sparrows, and the blue jays. Our paths would cross only slightly, but I could see the books getting thicker in each group. One girl, Jenny, laughed at me almost every day and said, "I read that book last year." In our circle I didn't talk, and looking at the pages made my head hurt and made me feel dizzy.

During reading I was so angry and ashamed I could taste my stomach acid come up into my throat and seep behind my nostrils any time I burped. I used to imagine killing the teacher. Mrs. C talked to the kids in the higher reading group differently than she talked to me. Her body language told them that they were "good," they were smart, and it told me that I was stupid. In my reading group each time I attempted to unscramble the words that floated around in my head, I tried to tell Mrs. C to let me stop. I couldn't breathe. I felt trapped. I was trying so hard and wanted desperately to be like everyone else. I learned that year to hide in the bathroom to escape reading out loud. In the bathroom, I would stare at the mirror, hoping to God that no one walked in on me crying. But it only worked sometimes. Mrs. C often stopped the lesson until I got back from the bathroom. When I returned, I could feel everyone staring at me.

I knew how important school was to my whole family. My

father was smart; my brother, Billy, had already left for college. My sister Michelle would go two years after him, and everyone knew that Kelly had tested genius as a kid. But Kelly and I had something in common. When I was in second grade, Kelly was depressed and missed almost half of her senior year of high school. We would hang out in the mornings, and she talked to me much like my mom did—about how school was intellectually and emotionally restrictive. She was an actress and a source of creativity in my life. But she would still go to college and get good grades. I didn't think I could do that. I thought I was stupid. At night, my parents argued about my school and about how much my mother should help me and how much of the work I should have to do. I sat outside their bedroom, and listened and heard the anger and pain in my dad's voice. I wanted my dad to be proud of me and to love me, but I didn't know what I could do to make him think I was smart.

About once a week I waited outside my second-grade classroom and listened to my mom argue with Mrs. C: "You are destroying this kid. Look at him. He doesn't shower. He doesn't talk. He has been diagnosed with depression. He's only seven. Every time you terrorize him with those goddamn spelling words, he wants to kill himself." I worked for three hours a night on my spelling that year, only to fail every test. "Kids have to learn how to spell. Those are the rules. There are no exceptions, Mrs. Mooney." So my mother created the exceptions: "mental health days." Anytime I had a spelling test or I didn't want to go to school, I didn't. "Screw Mrs. C and her stupid spelling tests. We're going to the zoo." Mental health days were one of the few bright spots in my life, when the pain stopped for a while. My mom and I just watched the animals and bought popcorn. Even as the afternoons would end and I would start to rub my eyebrow because I was so scared to go back the next day, my mom would say, "Fuck Mrs. C and her spelling test. You are smart, and they don't know who you are."

Those words were embedded in the back of my mind and have stayed with me.

The first day of third grade, after I asked my mom what was wrong with me, I met Mr. Rosenbaum. Walking into his room, I unconsciously rubbed the bald spot on my eyebrow and looked down at the ground. Unlike when I was a little kid, I was now afraid of adults; in school they made me feel ashamed of myself. Mr. R came right up to me before any of the other kids. When I walked into his classroom, he asked me what I liked to do. I didn't know what this man wanted, so hesitantly I told him: "I like to play soccer. I am really fuc. . . , I am really good."

He laughed. He had already met my mom and was familiar with my family's profound way with words. "I know. Your mom told me you were. They are really proud of you."

"Yeah. Well, my brother comes up from school, from San Diego, to watch me play and my sisters scream on the sideline, 'Kill them, get the fuc. . . , ah, get the ball.' My brother says I can be a professional, and my dad's my coach. He tells me I do a good job. Can I bring my ball to class?"

"I don't see why not. You just have to let me kick too."

"I play all the time, on my own. No one tells me to. I work really hard, I do. I work really hard, Mr. R."

"Your mom said you don't like to spell."

"Fuck spelling . . . I'm sorry," I said with my head down.

"Let's not worry about spelling. Who needs it anyway? What else do you like to do?"

I couldn't believe he had said that. I felt lighter for a second, and I smiled. "I like to build things, and I like stories. I like to read them, to look at the pictures, and I like to make them up. I like that a lot."

He looked at me and said, "Well, if that's what you like, let's do it. The soccer part you'll take care of; the building and the stories, I got. Sound good?"

Throughout third and fourth grade, Mr. R kept his promise

to me. He created an environment where I could be successful, and he did not make me feel ashamed of my struggles and weaknesses. His classroom was project oriented, and I thrived in social studies and science. For one project I invented a running shoe with springs in it, which got the highest grade in the class. While I experienced these successes, my weaknesses did not go away, but Mr. R approached them as challenges. In his eyes the solutions were simple: do projects; no spelling tests; use a computer for any writing; and my spelling never counted against me. I still struggled with reading, but in Mr. R's class, there were no reading groups. Kids went at their own individualized pace, and I didn't feel as humiliated.

Most of all, Mr. R respected me. When I struggled during reading lessons, he sat next to me and put his arm around me. *That arm saved my life.* One day toward the end of third grade, he asked my mom and me to stay to talk about my schoolwork. He let me be part of the meeting and wasted no time getting to his point: "You know, Colleen, Jonathan is so bright." I couldn't help but smile when he said that. No teacher had ever told me that before. "And I also know you've seen the discrepancy between his innate intelligence and his performance specifically in the area of reading and spelling. He is exactly like my daughter who is dyslexic. She's away at college. I think Jonathan is dyslexic."

The idea of having a learning-disabled son infuriated my father, but I was tested and diagnosed with dyslexia. I had no idea what that meant at the time. It was never explained to me, and the school told my mother that my spelling and reading problems would probably go away in adolescence. At home, though, I could feel my dad's disapproval. When I was first diagnosed, my father had refused to put me into special education. In his eyes, it was where retarded kids went.

But regardless of the extra help, I knew I was slipping behind. By fourth grade I was in the resource room twice a week to work on reading. At home I kept asking why I couldn't read.

"You're a late bloomer," my mom would say. The resource room was a drop in the bucket, a Band-Aid, when what I needed was a new environment entirely. Even Mr. R couldn't stop the snide and embarrassing looks my classmates gave me every time I left the classroom to go to the resource room. And he couldn't help that every time I left for the resource room, I walked down the hallway with kids from the gifted and talented program (GATE). As I walked down the corridor I passed each grade, one by one, in slow motion. Sometimes, for cruel fun, the GATE kids would ask me what room I was going to, even though they knew exactly which room was mine. They wouldn't wait for an answer, but just laughed and called me stupid.

By the end of fourth grade, my parents, in the face of what was happening at school, latched onto my success with soccer. For my mother, the game became a medium of class warfare, where I was better than the affluent kids from Manhattan Beach. For my dad, soccer became who I was, the place where I lost the stigma of special ed. For years, if I did not play well, neither one of them would talk to me for the rest of the day. But in fourth grade, regardless of the pressure, I still loved to play. For a couple of hours every day, soccer gave me the feeling of what it must have been like to be a smart kid at school. Playing soccer took me through fourth grade and into fifth and sixth, where I no longer had Mr. R's arm around me.

In fifth grade I was not allowed to use a computer, spelling tests were mandatory, and I had to read out loud in front of the class. The year passed by in a haze, with the background noises of my mother advocating for me at school, while my father insisted that I had to go school, that I shouldn't need any help. But every other Saturday night, all that slipped away. My dad and I drove to Anaheim to watch the Angels play baseball. At the games, my dad seemed to change. We always left early enough to see batting practice, and he bought us meatball sandwiches. That year my dad had put me on a "diet" for soccer, but during those baseball games he let me eat without worrying about the fat. We watched all nine innings together every game.

In October 1988, I found myself at the most exciting baseball game of my life. My dad had spent all night on the phone to get us tickets to the '88 World Series—the Los Angeles Dodgers versus the Oakland A's. I was in sixth grade then, and so much was going wrong at school. But that night at Dodger Stadium, it all slipped away—soccer, school, the pain. The Dodgers won the game with a ninth-inning home run close to where my dad and I were sitting. We just stood there and cheered for what seemed like all night. My dad bought me a shirt. I wanted to stay there forever. As we left the stadium my dad turned to me and told me he loved me. In less than a month, I would drop out of sixth grade.

I spent my last day in sixth grade in the principal's office waiting for my mom. I had no idea why I was there, but I knew that it had something to do with a story I had written the day before for English class. I had worked hard on the story for over a week. For a moment, sitting there, I thought that I might have been called to the principal's office because the teacher was so impressed by my writing. Waiting for my mom, I welled up with pride.

I knew I could write a good story, and I wanted so much to do it well, to let them know that I wasn't stupid. At home in front of the computer, I tried to write about King Arthur and the Knights of the Round Table. I could play my story in my mind, seeing all the visuals and hearing the different background sounds. But when I watched it, I did not have words to describe it. So when it was over, I looked down and there was nothing on the page. *"Only stupid kids can't write,"* I told myself. I tried again. Three hours later, I stopped, and all I had was a page that was completely unreadable. I decided to ask my mom if she would write down what I said to her. I felt ashamed of myself and felt my father's eyes peering down on the work. But when it was all done, it was a damn good story.

When my mom arrived outside the principal's office, I knew something was wrong. In the office were my teacher with my story and the principal. With a piercing gaze, my teacher looked right through me to my mom, with a disgusted look on her face. "Did you let him copy this from a book?" she asked.

My mom answered, "How dare you!" I felt like I was going to vomit.

"You know, Mrs. Mooney, this is a very complex and intelligent story. I know Jonathan couldn't write anything like this. You know how he spells and what his handwriting looks like."

After being accused of plagiarizing the story, I left sixth grade for good.

With no school, all I had left was soccer. I turned my natural energy to getting better and spent the rest of the year practicing every day. But at this point, playing soccer had become much more complicated for me than simply being a kid who loved to play. The images of my mom on the sidelines, screaming at me while I played, haunted me. My father adopted soccer as his job in the family, and he coached my teams. He was obsessed with eating right, training, and sleeping, and I adopted his rituals as my own. The irony in all of this obsession and ceremony is that over time, they undermined my belief in my own skill and talent. I was terrified that my only skill would vanish one day. In the end, this regimentation took away my love for soccer, a game that had brought me joy and that I had excelled at. But by the beginning of seventh grade, it was all I had, and in my eyes, it was my only hope for my future.

I thought that if only I had another chance, I could change. In seventh and eighth grade, I got that chance. My new school, Hermosa Valley, was a small community school, and when I arrived, I made a lot of friends very quickly. I did not receive special accommodations, but unlike in fifth or sixth grade, my teachers allowed me to use the computer for writing and never counted my spelling against me. Reading was no longer a "subject"; I did it all at home, slowly (and poorly), but at that point in my life, I had memorized most of the words that I saw, and anything I didn't know I skipped. I thrived in social studies and science, which had projects as the core component of the grade. In eighth grade, I did a two-month project on evolution, and it was so well received that I presented it to a Kiwanis Club. I also took some real risks and enrolled in a speech class—not speech therapy like in elementary school (I used to talk like a Brooklyn cab driver), but public speaking.

By the middle of eighth grade, out of nowhere, I told my parents I wanted to apply to a private high school. This school required an admission exam, and I enrolled in a tutoring program to prepare. I told people that the school had a good soccer team. But underneath that surface explanation, the last year and a half had given me an opportunity to see myself as more than a soccer player. It was a month before graduation when I received my rejection letter. I sat on my garage floor holding the letter, crying. My mom came and held me. I had tried so hard to get in; I wanted so much to feel smart. But I picked myself up from defeat, and a week later, by submitting a speech that I wrote, I was chosen to be the graduation speaker for my eighth-grade class.

Applause erupted when I finished the speech in front of a thousand people on graduation night. Parents and even my friends told me how moved they were. The speech was simple. We all were standing on the threshold of our lives, I said, and we had the opportunity to really find out who we were and what we wanted to be. And I was grateful for that opportunity because I had struggled with learning, with reading, and I had changed at Hermosa Valley.

On August 10, 1992, I walked into the offices of my new high school in Lakewood, Colorado, to meet with Mr. Towner, my guidance counselor. It was the summer before my sophomore year, and my family had moved to Colorado in the middle of my freshman year. My first year of high school was like a flash-back to fifth grade. I was one of a few freshmen ever to make varsity in the school's history, but in a hostile school environ-ment where I received no accommodations, I got C's and D's, and I stopped going to school a month before the semester was over. We then moved to Denver in February. At school, I found myself hiding in the bathroom during my free hours and rub-bing my eyebrows raw. I failed or got an incomplete in every class that year. That summer, I devoted myself to soccer. By the time I walked into Mr. Towner's office, I had made varsity, the only sophomore starter in the history of the school.

Mr. Towner and my mom talked for a while and came to the same conclusion about how to manage my "learning prob-lems." Their conversation was mostly rhetorical, because Green Mountain High School had only two modes: a room for kids with mental retardation or emotional disabilities and the normal classrooms. About halfway through their conversa-tion, though, he stopped and looked at me in a way that made me not ashamed but sad. He asked me what I liked to do. His kindness reminded me of Mr. R, but I didn't tell him I liked to build things, and I didn't say I liked stories. "I like to play soc-cer." I said. "That's it?" he asked. "Yep, pretty much. I play soc-cer." I would learn my senior year that Mr. Towner left that conversation giving me a fifty-fifty chance of graduating.

Mr. S, my sophomore English teacher, did not buy my lie for a second and didn't allow me to believe it either. He was the guru of the English department. The first day of class, we were handed what was known infamously as the "The Big Chief"— essentially a journal we had to hand in every week for his re-view. It terrified me more than anything I had done in high school. My handwriting and my spelling would be out there to be judged by a man whose demeanor, arrogance, and detached intelligence reminded me of my father.

After I handed it in, I shrank away, but after class he asked me to stay. "Mr. S, I have to go to soccer practice. I am really sorry about the spelling, and I know I have bad handwriting. I tried really hard, I did." He looked at me and smiled. He knew I was dyslexic, and in fact I was the most extreme case he had ever seen in his teaching career. "Don't worry about it. I wanted to tell you that spelling and that stuff doesn't count. All that matters is doing the writing. Just write." A week later, after turning in our first written assignment, Mr. S would pull me aside again and say, "Your mind is quicker than your pen. I know that. You're so bright, and all that matters in your writing is those ideas. The rest is technical." He accepted me and reignited a passion I had always had for literature.

At the end of my sophomore year, many of my patterns had returned to haunt me. It had been a hard year. Weeks before the end of the first semester, I went into hiding, using a soccer injury to miss those last few weeks of school before Christmas break. I got two D's, a C, and one B in Mr. S's class and was so ashamed that I hid my report card from my parents. But Mr. S's class was different. At a time in my life when I was quickly becoming stereotyped as an athlete, his class connected me to a creative and passionate part of myself. For the second semester, I made a deal with Mr. S that if I improved and got an A, my grade from the first semester would change.

On the last day of the semester, I walked into Mr. S's office to pick up the two final projects that we had worked on all year. One was "Big Chief." The other was a project of his design called "The Web": a visual and spatial design representing all our work, connecting them together with ideas, emotions, and personal writing. The web was a picture of how my mind worked on paper. I got an A on both, giving me an A for the year—my first ever. That day in his office I said, "I want to be a writer." Like I was with soccer as a kid, I was determined to work hard at writing. "I want to be a better writer, Mr. S." "Then write," he said. "Join the newspaper, apply for honors

English, and write." Both of those were huge risks for me, but I decided to do it anyway.

Honors English was an exclusive little clique that I joined a week late off the wait list, after I was originally rejected. I was rejected not on the conceptual merits of my essay, but because I scored low on technical ability. As always, my mom and I went down to the school, and my mom fought to get me in. Standing outside the classroom, I heard my mom screaming at Mrs. S much as she had done with Mrs. C.

Mrs. S was the leader of this exclusive club. The first day, she told a story about when she first met her husband. He refused to date her until she'd read all of J. D. Salinger's books. She took pride in this fact. As the other students massaged her ego by laughing and reflecting her eccentric nature back to her, I sat in the back of the class, nauseous, nervous, and retreating inside myself. These students had been tracked to be in honors. I could see it in their posture and hear it in their voices. Many of them had been in honors programs together since third grade. They had been told their entire lives that they were intelligent, gifted, and bright. I wanted to be like them, but I simultaneously hated them with a passion.

That same week I joined the newspaper, the *Ram Page*, and met Laura, a cheerleader with blond hair and blue eyes and a near-perfect GPA. In many ways, she embodied all the things I hated but wanted so badly to be like. Later that evening, I got her number from information and spent three hours dialing and hanging up, until I finally had the courage to speak. I told her I was calling with "official *Ram Page*" business (I was a pretty smooth talker). By the end of the year, she was my girl-friend and my best friend. She was the only person who really knew me. She knew I had grown up in the resource room, and we joked about my spelling and reading. She was the only person I told about my dreams of being a writer. Soccer went well that year. I made All State, and everyone talked about my future, but she was the only one who knew how much pain it was causing me. At the end of the year, after a game, she turned to me and said, "Jon, who cares about soccer? You know I'll love you whether you play or not." She was the only person who had ever said that to me in my life.

In spite of Laura's support, by the end of my junior year, things seemed to be breaking up and speeding out of my control. I was angry. The SATs were approaching, the pressure of college was building, and classes were going poorly. But I put all of myself into honors English to validate some creative part of myself. I talked with Laura all year about ideas, literature, and my writing, but in class I kept silent. The kids in the class thought that they were the next James Joyce or Virginia Woolf, and the feedback they got all year supported their assumptions. I didn't do as well. The entire class consisted of in-class essays, a preparation for the AP (Advanced Placement) exam. Just like elementary school, every day of the semester I walked into that class to face failure. Mrs. S would later tell me that she knew how hard it was for me to participate, how risky it was. But she didn't care. I had agreed to be in the class, and I had to play by her rules. Mrs. S did not see my writing the way Mr. S had. I wanted to tell all of them that good handwriting and spelling and following the rules of some pathetic high school English teacher did not make them smart. But the most frightening thing that I grew to understand that year is how intelligence is a construct, and the rules of that environment, where form is the gatekeeper to content, did make them smarter than I was.

In December of my senior year, I sat in the office of a sports psychologist and thought about killing myself. I was at the psychologist's office, however, not to talk about my emotional pain but to talk about how I could perform better on the soccer field. By December, dreams of big Division I soccer scholarships were gone. I was deep in a slump that began over the summer at a critical Olympic development tournament, with all the college coaches in attendance, which was followed by the worst high school season of my life. With things falling apart, my father took it upon himself to drum up collegiate interest in me. He carted me off to schools across the country to meet with coaches who had no idea who I was, or those who had seen me play and were not interested in recruiting me.

On Christmas Eve, I was up early to spend the day with Laura and my mom at the zoo. I always loved going to the zoo to watch the animals with my mom. I wanted to share that with Laura. I felt so inadequate compared to her. I was resentful of her academic success, and I was destroying our relationship. But at the zoo, the anger I had inside went away, and I got a glimpse at things in my life that I was proud of. I was a peer counselor at the school, selected by Mr. Towner out of one hundred students, and I worked with eighth graders at a local middle school. I also was in AP English, where I struggled but kept writing, and started writing stories on my own. But just when I could see the positives clearly, the fake recruiting trips and the shrink made me feel that soccer was all that mattered to people. I felt ashamed because I wasn't a good player anymore, and I had let everyone down. I kept pushing, and they kept pushing, when all I wanted was someone to tell me to "fuck soccer." But there were no mental health days for soccer.

On Christmas Eve my mom, Laura, and I watched the Christmas lights. Laura put her arm around me and for a minute I started to cry. "What's wrong?" she asked me.

At 4:30 in the morning on July 20, 1995, I called my mom from the Jefferson County Detox Center and told her I was spending the night at a friend's house. I was so drunk the room spun around in circles. When I drank, the little boy who had to hide in the bathroom his whole life came out, broke free. I was no longer a minor, and after being arrested for public drunkenness I was stripped naked and given blue slippers, a hair net, and a white cotton gown. I was so scared and empty inside. I called Laura, who was in Boston. "Laura, I don't want to waste my life, do you know that? I . . . I . . . I don't want to waste my fucking life."

I spent the rest of the summer pushing through my difficulties with reading and continued to write creatively on my own until I left for Los Angeles. I had received a mediocre soccer scholarship from Loyola Marymount University, fifteen minutes from where my life all began, and where in less than a year's time, my life would change forever.

As we drove up the 405 freeway toward LMU, my past spun around inside me, and I was poised to repeat the same patterns that I had lived with for my whole life. I was at a critical turning point. I could revisit my past and change that cycle of self-destruction, or I could choose to do nothing and become a victim of my past. For the first few months of college, the spinning was almost too much. But I knew somewhere inside that, if I just kept pushing, it would stop and I could change.

*On the first day of soccer practice, two weeks before school started, I injured my ankle and was inactive for a month. All semester I called Laura late at night drunk: "You fucking bitch, you want to go where? Dartmouth? What makes you think you are so much fucking smarter than I am?"*

*The season went on, and my depression continued. After I recovered from my ankle injury, I made the starting lineup, but I was eighteen, weighed 135 pounds, and was playing against twenty-two-year-old men. A week later I injured my knee, developed chronic tendinitis, and was treated with cortisone. With pressure from my coach and my parents, I continued to play despite the pain. The day I injured my knee, Laura and I broke up over a pay phone in a Hilton.*

*By the middle of the semester, I had an F and a D, in part because I had not self-identified as a dyslexic student and had no accommodations.*

And then the spinning stopped just for a moment on, of all places, English class. The place in my life that made me feel the most inadequate. As soccer fell apart, Laura left my life, and I drank out of control, I went back to reading and writing. To say to the world, *I am more than you think I am,* I turned years of determination, anger, and sadness into fuel for working hard in my only English class. Mr. S had taught me how to write, and now I took that further, finding my own voice and writing process. I spent hours on the phone with my mom spell checking and then driving to Kinko's to listen to the hum of the fax machine late into the night. I put my soul into the writing. Heading into first-semester final exams, I had the highest grade in the class.

A month before winter break, I discovered that the final exam was an in-class essay worth 50 percent of my grade. I was stunned. Looking out the window, I felt paralyzed by images from the past. *Why I am stupid, Mom? Please, Mrs. C, don't make me take the spelling test. I work hard; I really do. I am smart.* My entire life people had advocated for me, made deals that my spelling wouldn't count, but most of the time I was terrorized by spelling. I didn't want to wait in the wings anymore. I had worked my ass off in my English class, I was a good writer, and I deserved to get a good grade in that class. In the back of my mind, my mom's voice rattled around: *Fuck spelling. They don't know who you are. They don't know who you are.* At the end of class I went to my professor. "I'm dyslexic," I said. "I need accommodations for the final exam."

A week later I was rediagnosed with dyslexia, validating my struggles with learning and my right to accommodations. The next week, I fought with a reluctant Department of Disability Support Services (DSS) for accommodations. They let me use a computer but gave me no extra time, and spelling and grammar were counted against me. I failed the exam. One in-class essay invalidated a semester of hard work.

The night after I finished my last final, I passed out in a bathroom at the University of San Diego after throwing up on myself. I started to come to terms with my past, but I was at the bottom of my depression. I spent December and half of Janu-

ary sleeping on my sister Kelly's couch during the day, but
writing and reading at night. That winter, reading literature
and writing poetry, I tried to stake a claim to something about
myself other than athletics. About halfway through the break,
I received my grades and got just over a 3.0—a huge trophy—
but given my effort and the fact that the lack of accommodations brought it down from what I thought should have been a
4.0, I snapped. Driven by the rage sitting inside of me for eighteen years, I struck out at the school.

The first day of the second semester, my mother and I
walked into the office of the director of DSS and demanded
that I retake my English final. The director looked at me
blankly and then flipped though my records. "You were accommodated for that test. Right?"

"Yes, but . . ."

He interrupted me. "Why did you not self-identify as LD in
your application to LMU?"

"I . . ."

He interrupted me again. "Why did you wait so long to approach DSS?"

I started to speak, but then he interrupted me one last time.
Looking directly at my mom and me, he smirked and said,
"Jonathan, what are you planning to major in?"

"English," I said.

"English?" he said. "Really?" he laughed. "Is that the best
major for you? Perhaps you should rethink that. To be an English major, you need to know how to spell, how to use grammar correctly, and you certainly need to be able to write. It
seems that those are your weaknesses. Perhaps you should
consider something, well, something less intellectual."

The next day I enrolled in four English classes. With the
same work ethic that I approached soccer, I faxed my papers
every night to my mom, pushing myself and my writing. I finished the year with two A's and two A–'s, the best grades that I
had gotten in my life.

On September 20 of my sophomore year at LMU, my team left for Las Vegas. The first game I was benched. At times throughout the game, I did not even know why I tried to pretend anymore. Although I had started the first three games of the year, my heart was in so many other places than soccer. I had spent the summer in Denver, living in a youth hostel, working as an organizer for the AFL-CIO. Soccer had gone to the sidelines of my life, and my parents supported my decision. It was a relief. But I wasn't surprised that once I got to school, soccer once again became the cornerstone of my identity. Back at school, I did not have the courage not to play.

I knew coming to Las Vegas that I would be benched. I had missed a road trip the week before to be best man in my brother's wedding. That night after the reception, for some reason, perhaps because of the rage I still carried with me, I told someone that I was thinking about transferring. So much had changed from just a year ago, when soccer was all I had in my life. That semester, I was talking about art, literature, and poetry. I had moved into an apartment and armed myself with a fax machine that hummed every night. I was successful, and it felt good. In the morning after the reception, transferring stuck with me. I found a *U.S. News and World Report* that happened to include "the US's Best Colleges" on my parents' bed, and I told my parents that I wanted to transfer.

Back with the team sitting on the bench at UNLV, the University of Nevada at Las Vegas, however, transferring was the last thing on my mind. Tethered to soccer was my sense of self, and I had no idea what I was without it. From the bench I could see the lights from the Vegas strip. I thought that I would have at least gotten into the game, but there were only thirty seconds left, so I started to take my shoes off. But then from the bench, directed my way, I heard, "Get in." "What?" I said. "Get in." I was on the field for a little over ten seconds. The ball was passed to me. I ran to it. . . .

I woke up on the sidelines. My leg was shaking and bleeding, and broken. My season was over. I took a deep breath, breathing in feelings of shame, anger, frustration, but finally relief. I had surgery on my leg two nights before Thanksgiving. I was done with soccer for the year and no longer had to make excuses for not wanting to play.

"The number is 272, no 274–71, no 7279. It'sss my sssister Kelly."

The officer dialed the number, and I prayed to God. I could feel the pain in my ankle where I had just had surgery. Finals were starting in a week, and I had straight A's. I had worked hard. I just wanted to go home and see the Christmas lights with mom and my sister.

The officer started to hang up the phone. "Is it the answering machine? Please let me leave a message."

"No messages."

"Please, she's asleep. She'll pick up."

He hesitated, and then handed me the phone.

"Kelly, Kelly, please pick up. I'm so scared."

I had started drinking that afternoon at four before a soccer banquet. The smell of the asphalt and vodka was still on my breath and clothes. "Please pick up, Kell. Please." I had been playing soccer for fifteen years. At 3 A.M. the police in the rearview mirror were a relief.

"Jonathan. Are you okay? What's wrong?"

The LAPD had held me against their squad car, searched me, and then cuffed me in front of fifteen of my friends. "I am so sorry. I'm in jail. Please pick me up. I am so sorry, Kelly."

She drove me to her house in the middle of the night. "Just run me over with your fucking truck. Just run me over. Please pull over so I can get out and you can run me over." I cried the entire night.

I had hit my emotional bottom but kept fighting, blindly, sometimes ignorantly, but always fighting. When I left Kelly's house the next morning, I realized that academic success would not cure me. I had to face myself with the same courage

I had faced my educational history. I committed to this battle as I did everything else in my life; it would lead me to years of therapy, recovery, and personal growth.

Christmas break of my sophomore year, I hit the road again, the angry red-headed boy stronger than ever. I finished the semester with a 3.98 GPA. It was time to make a change, and much like my brother who, without a job, moved to New York and changed his life, I wanted to head out east, where no one knew me and no one knew I was coming. I spent my vacation on the road, looking at top ten colleges up and down the East Coast. But this time, it was no one's idea but mine.

On January 3, I drove into Providence, Rhode Island, in the late morning. I finally found the school and then the athletic department where I had a meeting with the coach. I still held onto the idea that I was going to play soccer at school and had sought out only universities that had Division I programs. After seeing the coach, I found myself in the lobby of Brown's admissions office waiting for an interview. I laughed at myself. Me, a kid who could not spell his own name and who had lived in the resource room in elementary school, in the lobby of an Ivy League admissions office. It was comical, but I was not afraid. In the interview I told them who I was—my struggles, my passions, and my victories.

On April 1, I mailed the last of my transfer applications from the Fed Ex office at Los Angeles's airport. The spring semester had been filled with anticipation and a sense of change. I had identified Brown as my first choice, but it wasn't looking good. A week after they received my application, I was told that I needed my SAT II test to be eligible for admission. I had never taken those tests. I decided also to apply to Penn, Columbia, and Northwestern, where I was offered a soccer scholarship. But driving back that day, none of it really mattered anymore. I was frightened and excited, but I had put all of myself into transferring, and I had nothing left. There was no more hiding in the bathroom. Driving home, I knew that I was in for either a tremendous victory or a tremendous defeat. Either way, things would be fine. As I drove home, an almost joy settled over me. The opening of my application, a quote from a dyslexic poet who could hardly spell his own name, William Butler Yeats, ran through my head:

*I will arise and go now, and go to Innisfree,*
*And a small cabin build there, of clay and wattles made,*
*Nine bean rows will I hive there, a hive for the honey bee,*
*And live alone in the bee-loud glade.*

I knew that it did not matter where I went; Brown was not my Innisfree. It was only a place on a hill; it could never be anything more.

*"Then one day, in his own good time, Leo bloomed! He could read! He could write! He could draw! He ate neatly! He also spoke. And it wasn't just a word. It was a whole sentence. And that sentence was . . . 'I made it!' "*

Leo is always with me. He made it to Brown and has sat on my desk for all three years. He carries so much of my childhood. When I flip through the pages, in times of sadness or despair, I find joy. Leo holds all of those people who gave me valuable things. I remember Mr. R's arm, Mr. S, my mother's voice, my dad and the World Series, my sisters, my brother, and Laura. I remember joy. Because in the end, the wounds heal. The scars remind me of where I came from and who loved me; the gifts the people in my life gave me bloom the brightest and continue to grow.

# 2: David

This kind of writing has always been the hardest for me—when I really care about it and it isn't just a structure to be filled in. Because I do care about this. I want this to work together to create a picture of who I am and how I got here. I could talk it out. I know I could. But as soon as I sit down to confront the page, it all blanks out. (And that's if I can get past the resistance—almost a physical resistance—to sitting down in front of the computer.)

I want to let other people know how possible it is. I need to start by telling people enough about me so that they can put me somewhere where they can understand me without me being too far out of view—of them, of their kids, of the kids they teach.

So where do I start? Born, 1975; Hanover, New Hampshire. Public school until I dropped out at age fifteen during sophomore year. Ran away from home (sort of), did a lot of drugs (acid mostly), lived on the streets (in San Francisco for a couple of months). Then I came home, got sober, went back to school (at the Putney School), then off to Landmark College. Two years later, I was an academic whiz kid, and I transferred to Brown University, rediscovered my need to make art, and wrote a book. This book. Amazing Grace (short form): lost/blind; seeing/found. That is the simple version, anyway.

One thing is for sure: my story isn't a story about having a deficit of attention. I can pay attention just fine. I'm paying attention right now. (And I have been for a few hours.) I have played a single video game for eight hours straight, made art for fifteen at a time, and had sex for three. I can pay attention.

(And I know the response. "Yeah, to what he likes; when he wants to . . .")

What is that about, anyway? "He can pay attention to what he likes/wants to." It is definitely about living in discomfort. I used to be afraid to get my head wet. I would panic; it would overwhelm me. And in the pool at Storres Pool—my chest is tightening right now—and my frustrated mom. And uncomfortable, because other people are staring at her. And all eyes are pointing at her and it's my fault, *my fault,* that all of the people are disapproving of her. I just don't want to get my head wet. *"So does that mean that kids should only have to do what they enjoy?"* Maybe. But I had to get my head wet if I was going to learn to swim.

I made my first metal sculpture when I was four years old. In the back of the barn where my grandfather had his hobby shop set up, out of boxes of scrap steel, I made a toy race car. My father swears that I designed it all by myself and that all he did was weld it for me. He didn't teach me to weld for myself until I was eleven.

*First Grade: gold stars . . . a big grid with our names on it next to the door and a box of gold foil stars. I never got any stars. I forgot to be good to get gold stars until it was too late. I never got rewards for having lots of gold stars. I tried to not even think about the gold stars.*

When I was little I would sometimes slip into hopelessness/helplessness/resignation (not anger yet) just to avoid getting distracted. I would act crazy/crazy to avoid them finding out that I was crazy/bad. Acting crazy/bad was later. At least I was in control and could enjoy it.

I get frustrated by getting distracted. (That is a sane way of saying it; the better way would be: "badsitdownnnonotgoodagainalwaysneverdoitnotdoingitwhatyouaresupposedtodonow whatswrongwithyouwhodoyouthinkare.")

Ritalin? No pat answer or suggestion even as to where I stand on the yesorno of it. It's not yes or no to drugs. It is more complicated. Like, it's okay to give a child who needs pain medication some pain medication because he is in pain. It is not okay to give him pain medication so you don't have to read him a bedtime story before he can go to sleep. I was given Ritalin as a kid so that I would sit down at my desk more often in school. This was compassionate, I guess: I was punished less often for not sitting at my desk. I was able to wait my turn to speak—some of the time. This was also the use of a chemical restraint on a seven-year-old. Powerful psychotropic drugs were used to maintain order in an inaccessible and inappropriate academic environment. (And, no, blame can't be deflected onto the integrity of the physician. He is the head of child psychiatry at one of the best teaching hospitals in the country.)

Second grade: I was sitting there in the hallway and I was really sad and achy and I was back somewhere in my mind where I went all of the time; I felt cold and sweaty, and suffocating.

*"David! Did you hear me ask you to talk? Is it your turn to talk? How many times do I have to tell you before you listen to me? You are such a smart little boy. Why don't you act like it? You may not talk out of turn! All the other little boys can sit and listen to me. What makes you think that you don't have to?"*

*That ache around my stomach—a squeeze on the whole inside. Bad. Why to I have to be such a spaz all of the time? I hate being such a spaz all of the time.*

The custodian who was always walking around wore blue, wobbled, waved, rocked back and forth when he walked; he had cartoon black hair, he was quiet, and he didn't ever say anything to me. I liked him and he liked me. And Mike (I think that was his name) would say "hi" to me later, in high school. He still remembered me and knew my name; it embarrassed me. I wasn't embarrassed because of my friends. I was embarrassed because of me. I didn't want to be the bad-kid-in-the-hall again. Later, in sophomore year, when school was falling away (getting high, not going to class, top-of-my-lungs-arguing about black clothes, in-school suspension), I would go and hang out in the janitors' lunchroom and joke with him.

*Seventh grade: Mr. Plaut's math class, I became a needy, annoying know-it-all. I didn't interrupt to piss him off—at first anyway. In seventh grade you have to do your homework, or you fail. I had a 98 test average, and I failed for not doing homework. That is when my mom came in and yelled, I think. I don't remember it from back then, but she talks about it a lot—likes that story best. I didn't talk to anybody in seventh grade.*

I hated French class and wanted to be good at it. I swear I did. (I hear you thinking: "Then why didn't you do the homework?" I tried. "Yeah, for like five minutes. You looked at the page and then got up and didn't do it any more.") I remember sitting at the kitchen table, Dad standing over me. Sitting there not doing the work.

*"Middle school is about getting work done," my social studies teacher said solemnly one afternoon while standing over my desk after the other students had gone to lunch. "If you have the brains but won't do the work, then I can't help you." He paused for a second and added, "Hell, son, if you would just try, I'd help you along—which is a damn sight more than they're gonna do in high school."*

Jan the art teacher let me hang around, and it would be okay. I would walk out of math class sometimes and go into the art room. I didn't make any art (except for two little paintings and a batik mask), but I knew that she liked me. I remember everything she said about the color wheel and how colors look together.

Seventh grade was the worst year. By the end of seventh grade I had given up on school. I didn't have the guts to leave school until the beginning of junior year, but I was as good as gone by the end of seventh grade.

A hyperactive little kid born into a family descended from farmers (except my father, who's as bad or worse: hyperactiv-

ity shamed out of him—instead of taciturn, he's anal reten-
tive). No one talks about anything unless it is mediated by a
tangible thing. Being supportive means keeping you clothed
and fed. When I was fifteen I left home—dropped out of high
school and ran away. We have never had a frank conversation
about it. We drop an uncomfortable joke once in a while about
the "wild years."

But that's the whole picture. I come from a pair of unbeliev-
ably loving, exceptionally dedicated parents—one half from
Yankee farmers and the other half from New York Jews. They do
everything that they can, and they just didn't know what to do.

High school: I was thirteen. (That summer: IQ test, he-must-
just-be-bored, skipped over eighth grade and into high
school.) Perfected the disassociated nerd-robot-prove-it voice,
wore the same clothes every day—blue jeans and baby blue oxfords, no belt or socks. Nothing was out of control. I was in advanced classes, but could barely talk my way into C's. I didn't
ever do the homework or reading or labs, and had gotten past
the time when I could ace the exams cold.

The art room was the first place that I had ever felt comfortable—art projects everywhere and an expectation of "fuck
you." I rejected my blue oxfords for black clothes. Fights at
home started coming every day.

The first time I got high, it was as if someone cut off a
straight-jacket I didn't even know I was wearing. I stopped trying to follow the rules. I got high and felt comfortable. Drugs
gave me the ability to alter the world—to turn it into a place
where the effort I put out was just right.

Self-medication? Maybe, but also chemical self-acceptance.
I lowered my own expectations. And it came with a lifestyle,
and money, and rules of conduct. I became very good at bringing my standards down. School was irrelevant.

*In-school suspension: It's what happens when you don't sign
in when you are supposed to at the office. Signing in is what hap-*

*pens when you don't go to every class you are supposed to. Those are the rules.*

*In-school suspension happened in a small cubicle of a room set off the narrow hallway between the vice principal's office and the photocopy machine. Five feet wide and eight feet long, no natural light, no door. The only view was of the vice principal's secretary through a plate glass window on the other side of the hall. A small enough space to light with a desk lamp, but lit instead with a two-tube fluorescent fixture running the entire length of the ceiling. And a desk and a chair. Nothing was allowed except the doing of work. If I put my head down on the desk, the secretary would rap her pulpy knuckles on the window of her cubicle until I pretended to be awake. Periodically she would waddle over anyway and ask, "What are we supposed to be doing now, Mr. Cole?" I would never answer her unless ordered to, but I would always make a point to slam shut whatever book it was that she wanted me to open as soon as she turned away.*

*All day. Six hours sitting still. Winding up tighter and tighter for six hours. By the end of a day in that room, I had nothing left inside but blind rage. Hate. Six hours under lights that gave you a headache after two. Every teacher who walked to the photocopy machine clucking his or her tongue and looking down his or her nose. I spent six hours fantasizing how I would torture them if I had the chance. What was the outcome they were hoping for?*

I still don't have any real clarity on getting high. It wasn't a good thing, granted: addicted, self-destructive, nearly died, ruined my life and the lives of those around me, but it was the first time when I felt like I had taken a little bit of control.

My trip to California the summer after my sophomore year in high school was just flourish on the empowerment-through-self-destruction-trainwreck of getting high. All except maybe the decision to come home. I hit a bottom, got a sinus infection, and was sick. My hair was stringy, greasy, in my face, and smelled nauseating. Stopped and had a moment of clarity. Keep it up and die, or do something else.

Came-home-lived-with-my-grandmother-got-dragged-to-meetings-by-a-girl-got-sober-cleaned-up-worked-applied-to-school-private-school-the Putney School. Truthfully I don't remember most of it. After I stopped doing acid, it still took a year before I stopped hallucinating almost every day (and two years before my night vision came back, and four years before I could dial a seven-digit phone number without having to look at it three times). Found a group of people—sober students at the local college—and tagged along.

Yup: "those meetings." Insipid coffee, cigarette smoke, and some stale Oreos in a tin next to a gigantic percolator. Old normanwillybob crazyeileen sitting in the front row every single Wednesday. Some hope, some complaining, some God, some war stories. I fit in there. What people say there makes sense to me. My group of friends expanded beyond the handful of sober young people. Same meetings every week, no matter what. A ritual. Control. Unconditional support, a break, some perspective, a physical escape from school. Putney School, then Landmark College.

Five years in Putney. Spent my first three years at Putney flipping in and out of a "Fuck it, I don't care about any of this shit, this isn't important to me" and "I will take what comes." Needing to be prepared—a Swiss army knife, waiting for the shit to come flying, needing to know how to pull things off. I would make a better goalie than a juggler (all except the waiting part).

At the Putney School, the dean of students wouldn't expel me, the assistant dean of students made sure he wouldn't expel me, my adviser always smiled at me, and Frank, my tutor, made sure I got enough done to just barely not get expelled. They all kept believing that I was going to make it. Somehow I began believing enough to take the SATs and apply to college. A landmark, the big Special Ed room. But steps are steps.

*I may have graduated from Putney with straight C's, but I did*

*graduate. Hell, I was class speaker at graduation. Now I was
going to learn how not to drool in class—or at least how to wipe
it up all by myself.*

Landmark. The dean there had ADHD and lots of lists
(though you wouldn't know it to look at him). He painted really good, totally dead paintings. I mean totally lifeless. His
handwriting was the only thing with any life in it—scrawled,
alive, playful, and crazy.

Richa Gordon, my tutor at Landmark College, helped me to
make some academic progress. I would bring in discrete tasks
("Richa, I need to learn how to skim"). I finished my first highlighter when I was working with her. Actually used it without
losing it until the ink was all gone. It went on the bookshelf
(and by the end of the year, we had pasted a long row of gold
foil stars underneath it as well).

I learned how to write at Landmark—learned how to write
bad drafts, how to turn it into a game, how to beat it. I taught
myself how to outline with models, building papers out of
Tinker-Toys. I earned academic success, and it gave me the
confidence to go after more. I went back to making art, and
when our final English project was assigned—"Explicate your
writing process"—I responded with steel sculpture.

*On the table, a giant steel book lay spread open on a piece of
steel paper, spilling its contents of small brass ideas. A small steel
model set, an outline, a steel writing quill, and a steel inkwell, all
laid out with an exactness that mirrored the effort that it had
taken to develop the processes that the piece represented. I explained that the title, "Process," is from the Latin, and means lit-
erally "to move forward."*

I live with a different perception—maybe it wasn't so different when I was born, maybe then it was just a specific deficit
like the experts talk about—but by now, after twenty-four-plus
years, it sure is a different way of beingthinkingacting. I'm not
denying my weaknesses, but I'm not apologizing for them either. My world turned a little different the first time a nice

quiet civilized person thought that I was crawling a little too erratically and then let me know it.

*Acting out.* My dad's words. Hearing them and thinking them is still enough to make me feel the pit/lump at the top of my stomach—"you are acting out"—swell, and embarrassed blush and ache. Acting out. Being bad. I know I did it a lot. Why? Anxious? Frustrated? Lots of it is getting wound up in the moment—drinking the whole moment and sticking there. Not getting stuck exactly, though I don't really have an option, but sticking there like a record skips. Something inside that I have no control over (or truthfully, I have some control over it—quite a lot now—but would hide behind not having any control, because I was supposed to have absolute control). Acting out.

I know. "He's got some good ideas but . . . but math homework . . . but book reports on time . . . but lab reports and homework and studying and . . . "David has got some really good ideas but . . ." But nothing. Do you think it was punctuality and learning to wait quietly in line that got me into Brown? Do you think it is how the world works that someone like me gets here? Here I am now, though, on the other side of this page.

I go through Landmark by turning emotionally laden academic tasks into paint-by-numbers exercises. I had developed some reliable academic skills, and suddenly it seemed as if there might be life after Landmark.

*I was nervously shuffling through a stack of college catalogs and transfer applications with my friend Karen. I asked uncertainly, "Do you think I can do this?"*

*"If you do what I tell you to."*

*"How much should I tell them?"*

*Her response was with her usual compassionate matter-of-factness: "How much do they need to know?"*

*A quiet "Everything" was my only reply. It was hard to believe that the play-by-play retrospective on an ADHD, high school dropout, juvenile delinquent, recovering drug addict was really what they meant by, "What in your life has prepared you for the college experience?" I had decided to pull no punches. If they turned me down, at least they were going to know what they were missing.*

*Two weeks later, I lifted a heavy cardboard box out of the trunk of my car and walked into the admissions building at Brown University. In the spacious waiting room, once the living room of a Victorian house, I carefully cleared off the coffee table. I started removing the items from the box, and before I had them even half set up, I realized that I was being watched. A passing admissions officer, weary from the final rounds of freshman applicants, was engrossed, watching me, a young man in a proper blue blazer, kneeling down on the carpet and setting out an assortment of welded steel sculptures on his coffee table. It was my "writing process." I stood up, introduced myself, and began to explain what I had brought with me.*

*By the end of the day I had cleared off two more coffee tables— in the office of the dean of disability support services, and in the office of the chair of the Art Department.*

Not your average college application story, but then again, I've never been much good at being average.

# 3: Institutionalized

On August 10, 1997, we unknowingly sat across from each other at the opening night of transfer orientation at Brown University. Two kids who were supposed to be a pair of statistics, now Ivy League college students. Next thing we knew, we had paired off and stood next to each other reading off a list of "wacky facts"—an icebreaker where each student had to guess what his peer's fact was. About halfway down the list, Dave read: "I didn't learn to read until I was twelve"—Jon's not-so-funny fact. And then Jon read: "I learned to weld when I was eleven and dropped out of high school when I was sixteen"—Dave's less-than-stellar fact.

At that moment, we both knew something about the other that was hidden to the world. Throughout our lives, we had looked to the idea of succeeding in school to define our worth and our intelligence. In childhood, we were told we were defective goods, and to be better we had to be other than what we were. In our adult lives, we tried to use academic success to define ourselves. In both of these situations, however, we fought a losing battle. Regardless of whether we were trying to fill up our holes or looking to be told we were whole, this thing called academic success still held our identities in its grip.

As we would learn that semester, after growing together as friends, arriving at Brown was not the end of our struggles. Arriving at Brown was in fact the beginning of a profound new challenge—the challenge of moving beyond "academic success," to truly using our education to redefine our selves and find personal empowerment.

In order to achieve that, we had to come to an understanding of how institutionalized education affected us. Recognizing how institutionalized education affects all of us allows us to take concrete steps toward becoming personally empowered and ultimately frees us to find academic success for our own reasons and our own goals.

In this chapter, we take a critical look at the oppressive nature of institutionalized education. First, we look specifically at how everyone suffers losses during their trek through the institution of education. Then we turn to the present and explore how becoming personally proactive is the first step toward taking ownership of your education. We explore some concrete tools that will give you control over your environment. Then we introduce our study skills, and explore how they can empower you to revolutionize your higher education.

## INSTITUTIONALIZED

Alexandra is in third grade and lives in LA in an apartment complex across from Jonathan's mom. After Alexandra's third week of third grade, Jonathan's mom, Colleen, ran into her in their complex. Unlike her normal greeting, a dance and smile, Alexandra looked very serious. She sat down quietly, with her head down. Colleen asked what was wrong. "I don't get stars on my math homework," she said. "All the other kids get gold stars on their homework, Miss Mooney. I study all the time. I just don't get that stuff. What's wrong with me?" Alexandra was not LD/ADHD, just a little girl, but she suffered the same losses we suffered. From the simple task of doing math problems at the age of nine, she had been taught that there was something inherently wrong with her.

Her experience is not at all uncommon. There are very few people in this country who escape their education without leaving behind some hostages. Our experiences are not the aberrant stories of two cognitive freaks, but rather narratives from a battlefield that consumes us all, like Alexandra.

This section briefly goes back over our stories to provide insight into an educational institution that takes something from everyone. Our goal is to face our personal losses with courage—not to allocate blame, not to play educational reformers, not to influence policy, but ultimately to discover what we want to change in our lives now and how our higher education can do that for us.

## A Case Study

The day we were diagnosed as "disabled" is one of those memories that burns too bright ever to go away. It sits at the core of our identity, bridging our consciousness and our subconscious, holding the key to our development, and it flickers like the buzz of a white fluorescent light bulb. This flickering light, however, not only gives us insight into the LD/ADHD experience, but also illuminates the educational system that affects all of us. In the end, the biggest challenge for us was not overcoming our weakness as LD/ADHD thinkers but transcending the biases and oppression of the institution of education.

Our case study starts when we are in third grade, when all kids want to be the same. But we find ourselves pulled from the group and sitting in front of two "doctors." At least that's what our moms call them. They might as well have had white coats on and dragged us from our classrooms in front of the other kids, because we knew something was wrong. We knew it had something to do with us not being "smart" and "good," words the teachers used when they thought we weren't listening, or when they yelled at us in the hallways. We were being tested in our minds because we were stupid and bad—not merely different from the rest of the kids, but much worse.

And then the testing began, for varying amounts of time. A standard children's intelligence test, a battery of other IQ tests, and the infamous Rorschach, where all the images looked like weapons or darkness. It didn't matter that the test gives both an average total score and a breakdown of subtests, and that each of us was dramatically above average in intelligence. What mattered was that on our subtests, the results were spiked—some abnormally high and others abnormally low. And following an established clinical protocol, this type of scatter pattern, equaling a standard deviation, along with other variables in the subtests, meant we were LD/ADHD.

Despite our intelligence, despite the areas of profound strengths that were in fact vastly superior to those of our peers, we became simple and easy to understand. We knew it all along, but it now had a name: "chronic disorder of the central nervous system" and a "chronic disorder in one or more of the basic psychological processes involved in understanding or in using language, spoken or written." And . . .

And then we found ourselves back in the classroom, in the environment where we failed to begin with. But it was no longer the environment's fault. As the "diagnosis" showed, the problem was within us. And they were even nice enough to give us a special room away from the normal kids for some of the day. In one way, it was the logical thing to do. As a medical diagnosis, LD/ADHD identified a problem or a disease in isolation. It did not matter that our testing showed we were abnormally strong spatial and logical thinkers. That would make things too complicated. The diagnoses identified a disease of the mind, and no possible strengths could result from a disease of the mind, could they? (Just ask Professor Russell Barkley. This "defect" logic is at the core of his belief that ADHD is an inherent deficit.) Again, it did not matter that we showed strong alternative learning styles such as tactile kinesthetic learning and artistic abilities. But these strengths were ignored, and we lost the chance to learn in ways that suited our cognitive differences.

Ultimately our diagnoses and the subsequent attempts at intervention allowed people to blame us, two powerless kids, for our failure instead of turning a critical eye toward the environment. It took us fifteen years of personal and academic struggle to stop blaming ourselves, to stop believing that we are inherently defective like "they" thought, and to come to realize how profound an effect the environment had on our inability to succeed. Only as time went on did simple interventions like the ability to get up out of our seats, the use of a spell checker, and progressive ideas like project-based learning and other modifications to the learning environment allow the pathology to slip into irrelevance and enable us to be successful.

Our hard wiring is a simple cognitive difference. We all have them. But an oppressive educational environment that blames children for their failures caused us to grow up with the stigma of pathology. We learn differently, and our success at Brown illustrates that we always had these alternate learning styles and were never defective. We faced a punitive educational environment, fanatically concerned with socializing behavior, and we fought against an idealized conception of normalcy, not an inherent life-threatening disease in our head. Our stories as case studies force all of us to look outside, toward the institution of school, to understand what we all lose in our attempts to become educated.

### Looking Outside: Past Self-Blame for a Better Understanding

We spend the vast majority of childhood in school. Our politicians and intellectuals debate issues such as vouchers versus charters, but no child is ever encouraged to question why he or she is in school. On the margins of our schools are the outsiders: the art punks, the drug addicts, and the losers who challenge and criticize the codes of school, its function, and its importance. Many teachers and reformers ignore these kids, writing them off as angry, misdirected punks from bad families whose parents, or the media, are to blame—or that ultimately the kids themselves are to blame. These messages are ignored because they threaten a core concept of cultural power; they threaten our blind belief in the objective nature of education. But when the kids bring guns to school, we finally listen. When something as horrific as Littleton occurs, our society, appropriately, turns its critical lens on social sources, such as the media, the parents, and gun control laws. But no one has had the courage to look at the fact that those two kids at Columbine High School wanted not only to kill themselves and their peers but tried to blow up their entire school by wiring it with explosives.

No blanket statements will ever be absolutely true about our schools, and no single teacher or school district is to blame, but education is an institution, and there are common threads in all of our experiences. We are not taught to look with a critical eye at our education. We all face a system that has oppressive elements along with virtuous ones, and we all experience a level of sacrifice and loss. By looking outward and exploring our schools' function as a socializing institution and the values underpinning its structure, we can come to a better understanding of ourselves in an effort to change our future.

### Socialized

One of the most devastating things we faced was the unspoken reality that school is fundamentally an institution charged with socializing kids. By *socialize,* we mean the function of school is to shape the behavior and thinking of children and give us identities that fit cultural norms. Our elementary schools were institutions of discipline and training, and only secondarily places of learning. We see it in the third graders we work with in Project Eye-to-Eye, our program that matches LD/ADHD college students with LD/ADHD elementary school children as role models, tutors, and mentors. No one ever asked them how they feel, but when we do art projects, images of fear or anger and repression rise to the surface of their poetry.

We experienced the same emotions as kids. The moral connotations of our childhood were almost unbearable. Unlike preschool, first grade become a place about conformity and following rules. These rules controlled how we engaged with our bodies, with our appetites, with other kids. We got little desks and were told we had to raise our hands before we could go to the bathroom, play, eat, or touch other kids.

Along with rules comes enforcement, a punitive system of punishment and rewards. Little kids learn to live in fear of getting their names on the board three times, ultimately to be sent out into the hallway or to the little blue desk in the principal's office. The goal is to not rock the boat. We all learn to control ourselves most of the time out of fear, not understanding the reasons, and not understanding the toll our passivity takes on us. The by-product is a socialization centered on the idea of being able to control our behavior. Behavior becomes a social indicator of morality, marking which kids are good kids and which kids are bad, and the highest value is one of conformity, passivity, and obedience.

School is also charged with socializing thought—molding how we engage with the world, what we think about, and how we express ourselves. Using the "objective" idea of learning, our schools' goal is to produce smart kids, and the function is to identify intelligence and support it. But the concept of intelligence is varied and subjective, and in many respects misused in many schools. Children are identified by their ability to learn, and their intelligence is defined by who can learn best. Therefore, the means to assess learning has to be measurable, quantifiable, and standardized. In our early lives, this took the form of spelling tests, math problems, and reading.

Our ability to perform on these sequential markers was used in the larger paradigm of formal and informal tracking. Many teachers abhor the concept of tracking, but they must function in an environment obsessed with academic performance, one that demands some level of tracking. Neither of us was "tracked" (although special ed is a track in and of itself), but we were in low reading groups, out in the hallways during recess and during math class. Tracking occurs every day, when one kid is called intelligent, another average, another stupid in such simple things as reading groups, and the seemingly benign hierarchies in the classroom such as "the student of the week" or the "hawk" reading group.

For us, what was tracked was our ability to perform on concrete indicators, like when we learned to read, our handwriting, ability to spell, or do math homework. The underlying notion is that all kids develop at the same time in a linear, sequential manner, and if some kids cannot read early, they are not intelligent. This environment gave us an identity at a time when our personality was malleable, an identity that revolved around the teacher, the authority figure in the room. We did not question the rules and the identity handed to us. We were taught that sitting still and getting gold stars on our math homework were more important than art and ideas, and much more important than what kind of people we were and how we treated other kids.

In this environment, it is no wonder that many kids, whom many professionals would argue are natural learners, start to hate learning in elementary school and then come to high school bearing firearms.

### One Teacher, One Learner, One Mind

The core environmental challenge we faced was the structure, pedagogy, and value implications in the organization of our schools. In the vast majority of our public elementary schools, the teacher-to-student ratio is well over fifteen to one. Necessary to this structure is the idea that there is one right way to learn, and one right or "normal" mind. As a result, the vast majority of schools in this country value one type of mind, one type of intelligence, and assume a universal learning process for all children. This is one of the most devastating prejudices dominating our schools.

Over the past twenty years, Howard Gardner has developed the theory of multiple intelligences, a radical reframing of what it means to be intelligent, challenging the common notion that there is only one kind of smart. He asserts that people do not have one single intelligence, but eight multiple modes of representation. In his observations, schools support the development of only a narrow set of intelligence. In this light, vast parts of our selves—creative parts, intuitive parts, and emotional parts—go undeveloped. The arts are seen as extracurricular, and in many schools, they have disappeared entirely.

In addition to the concept of multiple intelligences is the separate concept of alternative learning styles, which challenges the common notion that all people learn the same way. Many educators believe that people process information and in turn learn in multifaceted and individual ways. Some alternative learning styles are tactile and kinesthetic, verbal, visual and spatial, and project based. Again, as a result of the structure of most schools and their underlying assumptions and values, our teachers teach to a universal learning process for all children: one teacher, one way of presenting the information, one way to learn.

Our inability to learn along a very narrow paradigm led to our label of pathology. For sure we had certain weaknesses (spelling, attention span), but we also had enormous strengths for learning outside the lines that were obvious when we were children, but went underutilized and were never valued by our schools. Not only were we labeled as diseased, but we also lost the opportunity to be educated in the most appropriate way for our individual minds. We lost our opportunity to enjoy elementary school; instead, learning became a struggle. Trapped as children by a narrow understanding of what it means to learn, we lost our passion for learning and our passion for school, which we had to fight to regain later in our lives. We also lost the opportunity to develop the intuitive, emotional, and creative parts of our minds. These were identified as irrelevant, as learning became about memorization and sequential thinking, and not about creative, intuitive ideas.

### *Your Report Card, Your Worth*

Most devastating for us was the highest unspoken value of school: grades. As kids, all we wanted to do was learn, to be with other kids, and be loved. School intervened in this process with a carrot tied to our academic performance and behavior. Our success at school—the way we performed and behaved—became who we were. Like Alexandra, we felt this at a young age and had no way to understand its origins. All we knew is that kids who sat still were good, kids who spelled well and read well were smart, and all that mattered was the competition and the comparisons. And every year the school issued a report on who we were. As Alexandra knows so well, success at seemingly objective tasks meant everything; it was who we were in a very real sense. Performing well became synonymous with being good and being smart. Academic success, which was supposed to be about learning, became a battle for our identities, and only the top 10 percent of the class could ever be truly whole.

It is important to take a moment to think about how school teaches us about our worth, because even the kids who fall in the chosen 10 percent suffer under this regime. We know this from personal experience. In our twenties, we still believed that succeeding traditionally was synonymous with being. From our first days in school, we are given an idea of what it means to succeed. It does not mean having compassion for the kid who falls down on the playground or questioning why we have to spell correctly. Instead, success means reaching for those gold stars at any cost.

We have come to know that just by engaging with all of these questions, by thinking about our past and the institutions we have come from, we have taken a huge step toward change. The key to using our higher education as a means for personal empowerment lies in demystifying the success, making it tangible, within our control, and then redefining success for ourselves and ultimately finding success on our own terms.

In the spirit of revolution, it is time to look at praxis: the merger of theory and action.

## Praxis: Taking Our Education Higher

We know you did not buy this book to theorize about education, nor did we write it for that purpose. The fundamental goal of this book is to give you ownership over your education and the tools to do what you want to do. We do not want to live our lives running blindly from old ghosts or bouncing on strings like puppets. And we don't want to waste this time in our lives trying to fix ourselves, playing out the narrative of a school system that sees diseases in weakness and squashes creative thought and individuality. College is an opportunity for you to define who you are, for yourself, to heal old wounds, and to get back anything you lost in the gauntlet traveled thus far. Let's get down to it.

Our first step is personal proactivity. Much of school past and present is about reacting to external pressure, other people's definitions of us, and other people's expectations of who we should be. Our first and biggest step to making the most out of this opportunity is arriving at a place where we look inward for direction to chart our own educational path.

### Proactive Past, Present, and Future

If all you want to do right now is to cram for an exam or blow off some work, you're in the wrong part of this book. No problem. Just move on to Part II.

What we are looking at here is how the act of self-reflection can be an empowering experience. Looking at your past, present, and future is not only good for the soul, but it also can be good for the budding pragmatist inside all of us. The stuff that you dig up in this section can be used for personal essays on any application, fellowship statements, job interviews, or just some good material for therapeutic writing. (It is also damn good for the sensitive guy/girl front.)

*Recovering Your Dead.* None of us escapes our past unscathed. However, neither we nor anyone else can claim to know where you come from—your victories, your wounds, or your losses. For us, going back over the previously unexplored territory called the past was a difficult, terrifying, but ultimately freeing experience. There are many different ways to do this, and no one is more right than another. We used a shrink (hereinafter called "shrink head")—check out your student health insurance. But one of the most effective tools was a personal narrative of sorts (a small example of the pragmatic value of this exercise: our journey turned into a book). What we did here was go back into the past like a reporter, interviewing all the major players. We talked to our parents, teachers, siblings, past girlfriends, and old friends. We also went back and looked at old pictures, school records, tests, and papers. If you decide to take a journey like this, here are some things to keep in mind as you search:

- **Have compassion.** As you go back into your past and find those ghosts, whatever they may be, have compassion for yourself and the people in your life. Try not to allocate any blame, or hate that little kid. Just watch. It is going to be an emotional experience that is about understanding, not blame.

- **Look for the story.** Look for what happened. Try to find those pivotal events—memories that stick for reasons you may not even know. Dig into those, dislodge them, and find out why they stayed with you, what was important about them. Also, try to put together a chronology of your life. If you dropped out of high school, what were the events that led up to that, and what happened afterward? Look for threads that go through it: the patterns, the ironies. This is the good stuff. Don't try to wrap it up in a nice, neat ball. The past is confusion, but there is power in knowing the course of your life.

- **Look for blood on the floor.** This is the most difficult part of the journey back. Find those wounds, and stay with them for a while. Think about times in school where you felt stupid, or crazy, or like an outsider. Look for things in school that made you compromise parts of yourself. What did you lose in your life? Who hurt you? What happened in school? What part of you changed? Who did you want to be? And in the end, know you can change these things, and have compassion for the little kid who lived them.

- **Look for the gains.** These are the good ones. What did you gain in your life? What did you gain from your struggles, from success? There are no wrong answers. Stay with these.

- **Look for lifesavers.** These are the beautiful people in your life who always believed in you and loved you: teachers, parents, strangers, coaches. Where were they in your life and what did they give you?

- **Ask big questions.** As you travel back and after you've got a little understanding of the story, go in for the kill. Why did you succeed/fail at school? Did you want what you wanted, or did you want what was expected of you? Did people pressure you and tell you who you should be? Again, keep compassion in mind. You can change these things, and knowing is the first step.

- **Find the joy.** Look for the joy in your past. It is powerful, and yet no one talks about it. Find it—whether it was a day, an event, or something you do all the time—and hold on to it.

*Living in the Present.* There is no way to avoid this cliché, but we do have a little spin to it. Taking an introspective look at our relationship to school today is itself an act of defiance. We are not taught to look inward for direction when it comes to school. We are supposed to follow the lead of the institution and accept many of its unquestioned values. The key is to look at yourself without judgment, as a problem solver and not as a moral legislator. Following are some things to consider examining as you stand on the verge of or in the middle of your higher education.

- **Assess your strengths and weaknesses.** To be truly successful in our endeavors beyond school and in our lives, the key is having the ability to assess our strengths and weaknesses honestly and objectively. We are all good at looking at weaknesses and ignoring strengths. Try to find the weaknesses, *and* put them in a constructive context. Figure out how to work around them, how to take their power away.
- **Check in and find your anger.** Take a moment to check in with yourself. If you go to a shrink head, this may be a good use for him or her. Just be honest. Are you pissed? Happy? Ready to get the hell out of school? Don't judge your reactions. Also, look for your anger. We all have it, and when you find it, try to use it as a tool or a motivator.

- **Embrace your creativity.** Many people hear the word *creativity* and think "art." But we're not just talking sculpture and painting. Creativity is a way of engaging with the world and a way of thinking that has nothing to do with the medium of art. Art is a creative medium, but there are plenty of other ways to be creative. What thoughts do you have that are creative? Are you a creative athlete? A creative mechanic? Find it in your life and hold on to it.

- **Think about taking risks.** Now this is a scary one, and huge. We are not taught in our lives to take risks, and we are taught to be afraid of failure. We are so frightened of failing that we hide and never risk anything. But it is only through risk that we grow as individuals and accomplish great things. Look for opportunities to take risks, and look for challenging environments. Know that these are risks and that the opportunity for failure is real, but also know that there really is no such thing as failure, only opportunities to learn.

- **Look for passion.** This is the fast track to the Buddha. Our passion for things, for life, for art, for anything and everything is what keeps us alive. To live life passionately is our ultimate goal. What are you passionate about? There are no right answers when it comes to passion. Just let whatever comes up be, and go with it when it takes hold of you.

- **Know how you learn.** This is probably one of the most important things to do when getting ready to jump head first into personal change. We all learn differently. Now, just for the sake of hypocrisy (a little hypocrisy now and then is a good thing), we could give you a standardized test, like many other books do, to assess your "individual" learning style. But to be honest with you, the best way to do this is to think about times where you felt really on the ball or learned something really well. Were you reading? Talking? Looking at an image? Or were you building or applying a concept? Jump into those times because when you know how you learn, you can learn and do anything.

*Imagining the Future.* This is our last stop, and we venture here with caution. Keep in mind that the future is not a place to live in. However, we cannot make any positive change in the present without the ability to imagine a different future. Set long-term and short-term goals, but look at these goals and the future almost through a hazy visor. You can see the horizon, but as you get closer, it keeps changing. Looking ahead is not about charting an absolute path, because we all know those are boring and are for linear people. But a life without moments of dreaming and looking ahead to the horizon, and imagining how things should be, for you and for others, is a wasted life. So look ahead with confidence and know that whatever you now believe to be true about your future will change—and that is a good thing, one of the best of things.

And now, with the shrink head stuff out of the way and a little buzz of proactivity, it's time to introduce what will carry the remainder of the book. These are the true tools for personal empowerment, academic success, and educational revolution.

### Power Tools for Personal Empowerment

Now you are standing either on the verge or in the middle of this "great" opportunity of higher education. You have gone over your past; you know what you've lost, what you want to get back. The bottom line is that your reasons for doing school are *your* reasons, and it is now our job to introduce the power tools, the concrete things to do for academic success on your own terms.

The biggest of these are our study skills, and they occupy the remainder of the book. We will introduce them in just a few pages. But first we have a few things to look at that make these study skills even more effective and give you more control over your education. The first is a new way to look at the institution of higher education, and the second are some concrete steps you can take outside the classroom to ensure personal success.

*Not the Holy Land, Just a System.* College is not an ideal holy land where perfect kids, with giant brains bulging out from the sides of their heads, engage in Socratic discourse in soft sunlight. In reality—and this is something we all need to think about for a second—college is not a single institution with a set of rules and expectations that everyone has to follow to be successful. Granted, it is a system that has its values and its codes, but it also has distinct parts, and so it gives us places to exert control. The college environment has resources that give you an edge, and there are things that you can personally do to stay in control. There is no shame in using these resources. On the contrary, find them and use them—they are good:

- **Tutoring and writing centers.** Every college has some variation of these. In some respects, they are not only an avenue to get supplemental help, but also a rare opportunity to personalize your education, and move more toward an individualized setting.
- **Psychological services.** The home of shrink heads. You know our take on this. Someone listens to you talk about yourself. If you're a born narcissist like we are, what could possibly be bad about that deal? But if on your travels you hit a storm, which you will if you are challenging yourself to grow and which we both have been through, and you need someone to give you some perspective, head on down to shrink head town. It is good business.

- **Academic accommodations.** For the folks out there with the bad handwriting, some problems with spelling, and maybe just a few problems with reading like Jon, and for all those crazy kids like Dave (you know who you are), these are for you. Check out the Reasonable Accommodations box and go get them—no shame at all.

---

### REASONABLE ACCOMMODATIONS

If you are a disabled person, you are entitled under some very powerful legislation to have the college environment modified for you. "Reasonable accommodations" (or "academic accommodations") are adjustments in the school environment to make the environment accessible to people with disabilities, including both LD and ADHD. An institution must provide requested accommodations that are reasonable in nature, do not fundamentally alter the nature of the course, and do not place an undue hardship on the institution. The institution is not required to provide services of a "personal nature" such as an individual assistant or a tutoring or coaching service (unless that service is also provided for nondisabled students).

Section 504 of the Rehabilitation Act of 1973 and the Americans With Disabilities Act of 1990 (ADA) are the primary pieces of legislation protecting LD/ADHD people. (A third, the Individuals With Disabilities Education Act, primarily protects children ages three to twenty-one.) We are protected as disabled people due to our "mental impairment that substantially limits one or more of the major life activities"—specifically learning. The ADA and Section 504 entitle LD/ADHD people to freedom from discrimination and mandate that institutions make "reasonable accommodations" to allow us to enjoy an equal opportunity to participate in all aspects of college life. Every school is required to have a Section 504 officer on staff—typically the director of disability support services (DSS)—who is responsible for preventing discrimination on campus. The ADA also specifically mandates that "examinations and courses" must be offered in "a place and manner accessible to persons with disabilities or offer alternate accessible arrangements for such individuals." This ensures that examinations measure a student's skills rather than his or her disability.

The DSS is often in a complicated and difficult position. At many schools, DSS is not an autonomous entity. Instead, the office is directly supervised and evaluated by the other offices at the college. This puts it in a bind politically: responsible to the law to suggest accommodations that can be very expensive to the college, but dependent on the college for salary and promotion. Sometimes the position becomes one of institutional damage control: making sure that the college is close enough to the letter of the law to avoid lawsuits. This is not to say that most DSS coordinators don't fight like hell for their students—most of them do. It is just a potential conflict of interest that students need to be aware of.

- **Deans and advisers.** These are your insider guides. Their job is to help you navigate the school. Use them. Talk with them, and often. Very few students take the time to develop relationships with these people. Ask them about their job, where they come from—anything. For the most part, they are kind, friendly people who want to help. If they like you, the more help they'll be.
- **Professors.** These are the fat cats with the grades in their back pockets. They can also be very interesting people with huge brains (sometimes). Build relationships with them. Chat with them. Tell them about yourself; ask them about themselves. A little chitchat can go a long way.

*Personal Steps*. We have a few more personal things to cover. They will allow you to create a more individualized, personal, and supportive environment:

- **Create networks.** Networking is a powerful tool, not just for suited-up squid boys (who just go with the current) preparing to go off to Goldman Sachs and Co. What we mean by *network* is to create a system that will allow you to share information and get information from a variety of different places. Identify important people—people who interest you for whatever reasons, whether it is that you respect their work, they're in your department, who cares. Build relationships with them, keep in touch, and send them e-mail (a good quick way to stay in touch).
- **Create cells of support.** In a time of personal growth and risk, it is important to identify and build relationships with people who truly know you. Not people who know only your faults, but people who know your weaknesses, your fears, and your dreams. These people will help you grow and are very important. We spend our whole lives looking for people like this. When you find one, hold on to this person.
- **Realize the power of emotional connection.** We've touched on this one a few times, but personal and emotional connections are very powerful. When you meet with deans, advisers, tutors, and professors, take the time to connect with them on a personal level, not just an intellectual one. Ask them about where they're from, their family, or just something as simple as where they went to school. Most people desire this kind of contact, but do not know how to take the first step. Take that first step. The benefits far outweigh the risks.
- **Get ready to get help.** This is our last one, but probably the most important. The ability to get help is a powerful thing. We know it's hard; we are taught at an early age that

getting help is something to be ashamed of. But getting help is a powerful personal tool, and not only a way to get better grades. There is no shame in it at all. We get more help every single day of our lives than most other people do in their lifetime. Jon's mom, bless her, still reads all of his writing, and he is twenty-two years old.

With this stuff in mind, it is time to look at the biggest power tool in our arsenal: the skills we use to find academic success that ultimately lead to personal empowerment and educational revolution.

### The Armory: Skills for Academic Success and Educational Revolution

When we first arrived at Brown, we thought that our challenge had been in getting in; but, no, it still lay ahead of us: getting out without losing our souls. You see, academic success had not cured us, had not fixed us, because there really was nothing wrong with us. However, fresh off the transfer boat at Brown, we still had to face the very real challenge of succeeding academically. For a while, we toyed with a traditional model, studying until our eyes bled. And simultaneously, as we went back into our past and explored what we wanted from college, we discovered that no one had ever really given us skills for academic success and personal empowerment. We had at our disposal only skills that had been developed by professors and teachers that were detached from the reality of being a student. Many of these skills were punitive; they tried to fix us and fit us more into some impossible model. Ultimately, all of these skills were based on the idea of one type of mind and one way to learn, and in the end were simply not good ways for us to learn.

During our time at Brown, we developed our own set of academic skills that allowed us to use our education as a means to

redefine ourselves. These skills and strategies take up the remainder of the book. The last question to be answered is: What
is it about these skills that allowed them to be revolutionary in
our lives?

*Beating the System.* First, and most important, all of our
skills are about beating a system. As we already explored, there
is a lot of social baggage caught up in academic success. Like
many other students, once we got to college, we slipped right
back into the elementary school mode. All that mattered was
getting those gold stars. But that is inane. Academic success is
not a reflection of our worth or our intelligence. It is a game,
albeit a game that has some positive aspects. The game is
about learning, and by playing it well you have the opportunity to expand your horizons. Also, playing the game opens
doors to your future and allows you to be who you want to be
in your adult life.

All of these skills come from the value-neutral place of beating a system that at times is unfair and oppressive. We address
honestly the fact that we do not do all the readings, we do not
study for exams ten days in advance, and many times we do
not take good notes. But we find success and learn nonethe-
less. These skills will give you control in this system and allow
you to chart your own path. They come from the trenches and
are about addressing the realities of school, not some mythical
ideal.

*Individualized.* Running congruently with beating the system, these skills are about you doing your thing, whatever that
may be. They are student centered and value the individual
differences that will allow you to do what you like without ren-
dering judgment. If you want to chill out with friends and blow
off a reading but not get screwed the next day in class, we'll tell
you how to do that. If you want to get a 4.0, study everything

under the sun, and then apply for the Nobel Prize, these will help you do that also.

Second, all of the skills embrace and value the individual ways we all learn. These skills do not impose a method for learning on you; they empower you to develop your own individualized process. Written from the perspective of two alternative learners, our skills are about mitigating weakness, reviewing and accessing information from alternative sources and multiple entry points, and getting more help than you can possibly imagine.

*Study Different; Learn Better; Be Sweet.* Here is the kicker: the same set of skills that allows you to beat the system on your own terms also leads to better learning. Many of the study skills books out there pay lip-service to alternative learning, but they still value only one type of mind and one type of learning. Our skills are alternative learning skills. In every section we explore multiple entry points to information, integrating color, verbal processing, pragmatic learning, and project-based learning. Follow these skills, and you will learn more than you ever thought possible, in less time and with less pain.

## The Coup d'Etat: Your Success, Our Revolution

Through the midterms, the finals, the tedious readings, your victories and your defeats, remember the ultimate power of what you are about to undertake. Living your life this way, on your terms, for you, and studying differently is revolutionary. These skills and this way of using your higher education are in direct opposition to many of those oppressive values we confronted in our past. This type of success outside the lines is an important message for all kids who suffer under those values. There are kids now who are learning to be ashamed of how their mind works or losing their creativity to conformity. By finding success outside the lines, for our reasons, we challenge everyone to reevaluate the standards we hold and judge people by. We force people to rethink how we define success, how we define intelligence, and ultimately how we define education.

# Part II: Schooled

# 4: Taking Notes Further

*If you expect to learn from lecture, you must take notes. You must, like the cub reporter of old, get the information down in black and white.*
WALTER PAULK, *How to Study in College*

## YOUR MIND; YOUR NOTES; END OF STORY

All of our lives, teachers tried to help us take our notes further by offering suggestions and advice in a similar vein as that offered by our friend Walter Paulk, an Ivy League professor. But to be honest, his advice and other advice like his, although well intentioned, is vapid and euphemistic, reminding us of common directives like "focus" and "take better notes." Neither one is very helpful for damn near anything. To cut to the chase, our boy from the Ivy Tower argues for what essentially is a standardized teacher-centered note-taking system firmly grounded in the idea that all students process, categorize, and organize information in a homogeneous and linear fashion: one mind, one note system. End of story.

Notes, however, are *your* tool to help *you* retain and learn information, and we all know that memory and learning are hardly black and white. The idea of simply getting down information in a homogeneous fashion fails to recognize that all of our minds are wired differently. For some, getting down the gist of a lecture is the best way to the path of memory; for others, the key to memory may lie in asking questions about the lecture or writing down connections between the lecture and a reading. For still others, the key to memory may lie in the structure of the notes, not the content. A traditional outline structure may be useless against the sea of ideas that rush to your head when lecture begins. This is our education, and we are anything but homogeneous.

The antidote to a teacher-centered, homogeneous note system is a student-centered, individualized note system that embraces the differences in all of our minds. While everyone was focusing on how we *should* take notes, no one ever helped us take *our* notes further. The bottom line: Your notes are *your* notes for *your* mind. Ignore anyone who tells you differently.

In this chapter, we look beyond the limited notion that there is only one way to take notes, and instead, in Section 1, explore how to individualize any note-taking system. In Section 2, we address the reality of lecture: a sea of relevant, irrelevant, and the "God only knows how relevant" information, and we outline concrete tips for taking *your* notes in an effective manner. In Section 3, we turn to learning from notes, and outline time-effective methods for reviewing them. Through all this, keep in mind that these are *your* notes, *your* classes. Take what is useful to you from our suggestions, and then blow off the rest.

Before we jump into the act of note taking, we do have one universal suggestion to make: Get a notebook. Although this may seem like an ideological contradiction (we are suggesting a universal system), there is a time and a place for good old pragmatism, and notebooks, an essential part of academic success, are precisely that time and place. They hold our notes, our papers, our homework, and our hard work in one reliable place. If you have a notebook system or don't care, skip on down to Section 1. If you do not have a system at all or are looking to improve the one you've got, try ours (well, the one we borrowed from Landmark College!) on for size.

This notebook system is simple: one notebook for each class, and each notebook broken down into sections or categories that make sense to us. No more, no less. We find it incredibly helpful to use either a three-ring binder or a spiral notebook as the core of our system. If you go with the spiral notebook, make sure it has a pocket in the front and built-in dividers. If you go with a three-ring binder, fill it with paper (our hands-down favorite is two-column law summary paper) and a set of dividers. Every three-ring binder also needs a hole punch. The plastic ones that snap right into the notebook for loose papers handed out at lecture are ideal. Set up the categories on your dividers either before or soon after the first meeting of the class. These standard categories are a safe bet for almost any class:

| | |
|---|---|
| Class Notes | Handouts |
| Assignments | Graded Work (tests, essays, |
| Labs/Special Projects | problems sets, etc.) |
| Reading Notes | |

We now have a single, organized, centralized home for each of our classes and are ready to jump into the act of taking our notes further.

## SECTION 1: INDIVIDUALIZING YOUR NOTES

The goal of this section is to help you individualize your notes. When your notes fit your mind like a rubber glove, the information from lecture is more likely going to stick. Also, knowing how to take notes in a way that best suits your mind bodes well for future endeavors. Storing and organizing information in the information age is a key to success. But the hard part about individuality is that there really is no bandwagon to follow (the individuality bandwagon, get it?). There are fundamental parts of any note-taking system that you can spice up with your own touch, but it has to come from you, from what works best for your mind.

To begin, grab some old notes if possible (if not, no big deal). With those in hand, we are going to explore ways to individualize the structure of your notes, your notation system, and your purpose and focus while taking notes. As always, if you don't care about individualizing your notes and all you want to do is actually take notes and be done with this business, skip on down to Section 2.

---

### NOTEBOOK BEGINNINGS

Creating a workable notebook system is the most important part of using one. Here are a few tips:

- **Keep it uniform.** However you decide to divide your notebooks, consider dividing them all in similar ways. If all of your binders have similar sections in the same order, staying organized is simpler.
- **Plan room for expansion.** A blank divider tab or empty section full of paper and ready to go can come in handy for last-minute changes in the course.
- **Leave well enough alone.** At times you may be tempted to reevaluate the structure of your notebooks. If a specific problem shows up—like needing to add a section for a specific project or study group—go for it. On the other hand, sometimes a complete structural overhaul seems like a good idea. (This usually happens when we are wide awake at four in the morning because we took our medication too late at night and *Green Acres* reruns have lost their appeal.) Survey says, "No good." Odds are that if you have taken the time to set up a reasonably good system, you have more to lose with a complete overhaul than you have to gain.
- **Achtung!** You may be thinking to yourself that since we are in the business of centralizing and organizing, the next logical step would be to just go get one gigantic three-ring

binder and divide it into sections for each course. We advise against it. One book lost one night in a semiconscious fog means one screwed college student.

## *Your Notes, Your Structure*

In elementary school up to high school, we did battle with the infamous Roman numeral system, with letters that did a little dance in our heads (Jon's head primarily) and with categories that never quite seemed to hold all the information thrown at us in any constructive way. How many times in your school career have you felt that category A for the main point was impotent against the sea of main points and subcategories thrown out at you? After all, there are a thousand main points, depending on how you look at things. Although we were given only one way to structure our notes, there is no one right structure for them. The key is to adopt a structure congruent with how your mind organizes and holds information. With an individualized structure, the act of taking notes will become easier, freeing you to get the important information down.

What follows is a list of ways to structure your notes and some comments on what is good and what is bad about them. These are ideas, not commandments, so take what you need from them:

- **Linear notes.** This is our least favorite of the bunch, but they work for a lot of people. To structure your notes this way, use a traditional roman numeral outline system. Record the main point and subpoints; add specific examples, each with a different letter, number, or Roman numeral. Consider this structure if you like to order things in a linear, hierarchical way using letters, numbers, or

Roman numerals. But if you think visually or spatially, these are not for you.

- **Two-column notes.** These are our favorite. The structure is simple. Get two-column notepaper or divide standard paper into two columns, and during lecture write down broad concepts, events, or themes in the left column. In other words, in the left column you are recording main points. In the right, you record specific information. This can be a description of the information in the left: names, dates, and other detail-oriented information. Two-column notes allow you to organize information using space as opposed to numbers or letters and allow information to move back and forth between categories. Intellectually, this structure is not yet completely nonlinear but is a happy medium appropriate for minds that think both laterally and linearly. It is good if you think spatially and visually but still like to maintain a little note-taking sanity.

- **Cornell guy's two-column notes.** You have to love this one. We bash the guy and then highlight his note-taking system. However, to be honest with you, Paulk has created the best traditional note-taking system we have ever seen. His notes are a hybrid of two-column notes and linear, hierarchical notes. Leave a two-inch margin on the left side of your paper and a two-inch bottom margin. During class, take notes in a linear fashion, in the center of the paper. After class, review your notes and write down key words in the left margin, and a summary of the notes in the bottom margin. This is good for all-around damn good linear notes.

- **Extreme notes: Mapping.** If you think visually or spatially and learn by looking at how information is connected, this structure is the ticket. To do a map, write the main theme of the lecture in the middle of the page with a circle around it and then let your mind go with the lecture. This is great for abstract thinking, but it can get a little confusing. It is best if you are concerned with themes, concepts, and relationships, not details.

Keep these structures in mind as the lecture rambles on. Experiment with these, and take them apart; try them all. It may take some trial and error to find the right fit for you.

### *Your Notes, Your Notation System*

In addition to the right structure, another key element to easy, comfortable notes is how you identify information and code it in your mind. You may not know that you have a notation system, but you do. All of those arrows, random boxes, and bizarre symbols that fill your notes are your notation system. A notation system is most effective when it is consistent and is used concisely. With your notes in hand, review the following ways to tailor your notation system. Again, keep anything that works, and kick the rest to the curb:

- **Use color.** Colored pencils, highlighters, and colored pens are God's gift to visual thinkers. If you think in pictures or if a block of one-color text seems unnatural to you, try integrating color into your notes. You can do almost anything with color. Try highlighting or underlining important points, or using different colors of ink for different ideas or to separate main points, subpoints, and evidence.
- **Use space and shapes.** An important key if you like to think of things spatially or visually. Try using an indentation method for different types of information: the more important the information, the farther left it is. Also, try boxing or circling information to identify its importance or separate it from the rest of the text. It's good to use color here also.

- **Use symbols.** A picture not only says a thousand words, but also saves you from writing cramps. Try using arrows to show connections or relationships. The most important symbol is the "red flag" symbol. This can be whatever you want: a flag, a star, or, for the artistically challenged, a bunch of frantic scribbles. This symbol marks the spot of a test question, an answer of any sort, a paper topic, or just something you thought was very cool.
- **Think about abbreviations.** Using abbreviations can be a very good thing if you struggle to keep up or if your handwriting looks anything like Jon's (i.e., not good). There are too many ways to abbreviate words to go into here. Our advice is to check out a book that lists abbreviations and choose a few, but always stick to what seems natural. An abbreviation system that you can't decipher does you no good at all.

Implement these tips any time, any place, and then move on down to the last bit of advice for how to individualize your notes: Your Notes, Your Focus.

### *Your Notes, Your Focus*

The traditional way of taking notes assumes that there is a set of information that you need to leave lecture with. That is only half-true. Although there are core pieces of information that should be taken down, there are different critical lenses to record it through and no fixed rules for getting this info, storing it, or learning it. Many of us learn not by simply recording facts, but by recording how facts are applied or how they are relevant to our lives. It's not that God ordained that the key to memory is identifying topics, subtopics, and details. In fact, coming at a topic from a different angle is the nature of what it means to be a creative thinker and dynamic learner.

These are your notes, and you need to learn your subject in

a way that works for you. However, if you take notes through one of the following specific entry points, know that you will most likely have to supplement your note taking with additional reading, reviewing other people's notes, or chatting with the professor.

If you want to take control of the focus of your notes, and take it out of the merely black and white, check out the following:

- **Question.** One of the most powerful ways to learn anything new is to question it critically. Your notes are no exception. If this is how you think, spend your note-taking time writing questions and identifying information. If appropriate for you, have the vast majority of your notes be in a question format.
- **Connect.** If you are an associative thinker, this may be the ticket for you. Associative thinkers make connections between ideas that to many seem unrelated. You know you are an associative thinker if you spend your time in class relating the lecture at hand to other readings, classes, or ideas. If this is you, don't fight it. Spend your time connecting the subject at hand to other lectures, other assignments, or other courses. Jot down quickly and briefly what is said, and then let your mind go.
- **Think conceptually.** Focus on the broader concepts, ideas, and theories that the class explores. This can be the place to do a lot of your thinking for the class. For example, Jon takes no notes at all on literal details, instead focusing on ideas that are sparked by the lecture or conversation. This means he needs to get the missing details from somewhere else, say, from reading, but he spends his time in class really engaging with the subject.
- **Think details.** The polar opposite of the conceptual thinker, many people focus on the details, taking close notes on all examples and subpoints and filling in the

broader stuff later. If it works for you, go forth and dive into the minutiae.

- **Think application.** Many people, including us, learn by applying information to the world or our life experiences. If you find yourself doing this, let it go. Throughout lecture, ask yourself, "How does this work? How does it apply to the world and to my life?"

- **Think emotionally.** All the good old professionals out there will tell you never to react emotionally to a lecture in your notes. Throw that advice out the window. Being passionately involved in the material is not only a powerful way to learn and remember things, but is what being a student is all about. When something in lecture pisses you off, write down your reaction; when it makes you happy, write it down. One of the biggest problems with academics is that they believe their work is objectively true and unencumbered by emotion. Stay with what makes the blood boil. It's more fun that way.

- **Think anecdotally.** Our minds hold information by storing it in a vast network of associations and relationships. Why take that out of our notes? If you find yourself recording seemingly irrelevant stories, don't stress. Keep writing them down. If it helps, go one step further, and note what your professor is wearing on any given day. Or note the number of hot members of the opposite sex you "find" yourself sitting next to throughout the semester. These anecdotes can be powerful tools for remembering the information in lecture.

Regardless of the focal point of your notes, the goal is to take ownership of why you take notes—not to conform to someone else's system but to get what you need, and in your way. With that, we have concluded individualizing your notes, and are now down to the dirty work: filling them up.

# SEVEN HABITS FOR
# HIGHLY DISORGANIZED PEOPLE

### HABIT 1: MARK YOUR TERRITORY

Every notebook needs your name, phone number, e-mail address, school address, and mailbox number written inside the cover or on the first page. Our books (including this one) have come back to us from points unknown more times than we can count because of this little precaution.

### HABIT 2: FIND IT A HOME

In the same way that it is helpful to have a central and consistent place to keep your notes, it is also helpful to have a place where you always keep your notebook. A backpack, messenger bag, or a spot next to your desk all work well. The key is to stick it in the same place long enough to get into a rhythm. Eventually you will develop the habit of taking the same set of materials to class.

### HABIT 3: PERSONALIZE IT

Choose and structure your notebooks according to who you are. This might be as pragmatic as associating colors with classes or scrounging binders at the Salvation Army. Also, go to town on your binders if that is a reflection of who you are. Spruce up standard binders and folders with a quick trip to the fabric store and a can of spray adhesive. (Think fake fur.) These items are going to be with you for a while, so it is worthwhile to build them so that you like having them around. Identifiable binders are also a lot more likely to come back to you if you leave them behind.

### HABIT 4: MAKE IT ESSENTIAL

Giving yourself reasons to keep coming back to your notebook is the surest way not to lose it—whether that means storing pencils in there, tucking some postcards and stamps in the back to fill out in slow lectures, or keeping a timepiece tucked into the front. Make the notebook essential to your life, and it will be more likely to stick around.

### HABIT 5: AVOID NOTEBOOK CROSS-OVER

Even if you accidentally grab your bio book on your way to psych class, it is still better to take notes on a loose piece of paper than in the notebook you have with you. Otherwise those notes are probably as good as gone. (Similarly, avoid the temptation to fold notes in half and tuck them into a textbook. Odds are you won't find them again until long after you need them.)

### HABIT 6: MAKE TIME TO DECLUTTER

Time spent maintaining organization is always time well spent. Once a week or so, sit down at a coffee shop with all of your notebooks and your book bag and tidy up. Every class-related piece of paper goes into the appropriate notebook. All of the rest goes into your planner to get dealt with or into the trash.

### HABIT 7: WATCH OUT FOR TRANSITIONS

Transitions between places or tasks are when stuff gets lost. A good habit to get into is doing a quick mental checklist of three questions: (1) Have I got all of the books I brought to class with me? (2) Did I leave anything under my seat? (3) Did I stuff any random papers someplace where I know they will get back to my room? (We also call this the "Class, Ass, and Stash" checklist.)

## SECTION 2: FILLING UP YOUR NOTEBOOK

Now that you have your note-taking system worked out and wrapped around your cerebral cortex, it is now time to look at actually taking notes. With pragmatic pride in our hearts, we fill up our notebook not to learn but to get good grades. But despite our good intentions, filling our notebooks is never as easy as simply walking into class, sitting down, in and out, and, boom! notes done. As we all know, what the professor says very rarely fits into those nice neat categories, and unpacking the lecture on the fly is difficult. Many professors cannot lecture to save their dingus, and most information in lecture falls into a gray area between extremely relevant and completely irrelevant. The key to taking notes is to know what's coming, who's giving it to you, and how to sort through the relevant and irrelevant and everything that falls in between.

### *Know What's Coming*

If you know what kind of information is coming before you step into lecture, taking notes is much easier and more effective. Knowing the topic of lecture is like navigating a dark room with a flashlight and takes less than five minutes. Here is how:

- **Review past notes.** Right before any lecture, take a few minutes to review the past lecture notes. (If you do not have them handy, skip on down to the next tip.) Skim them and remind yourself of the topic for that day. Also, pay close attention to the conclusion of your notes because often this is where the professor will set up the next lecture. If you find a set-up, read it closely.
- **Critically read your syllabus.** A syllabus is God's gift to holistic thinkers. The syllabus is an outline for the class, and each heading for each day is a hint about the topic for lecture. Read the course description first, and then the head-

ing for the day in question. Nine out of ten times, the topic
for the day's lecture is staring you in the face. Also, check
out the headings for the days immediately before and after
today's lecture. Taking a guess at how they fit together will
give you a broader context in situating your lecture.

- **Read a little.** Although it is tempting to blow this off,
  reading before lecture does have its value. Of course, we
  would *never* advocate actually reading. Nevertheless,
  skimming before lecture gives you a rough idea of what to
  expect from your prof.

Follow those simple steps, and you will have an idea of what
is heading your way come lecture. With that in mind, the next
important part to making lecture a friendly place is knowing
who's giving you the info, and how.

### Know Who's Giving It to You

Knowing the style of your professor goes a long way to making life easier in lecture—well, somewhat easier. Odd, isn't it,
but most of the study skills systems presented by teachers op-
erate under the assumption that all teachers can lecture well.
Unfortunately, this is not the case. Here are some of the most
common types of poor lecturers and some things we focus on
in our notes when we run into them:

*Type 1: The Rambler.* This is the guy who wanders from point
to point, without logically connecting them until someone re-
minds him that the class ended five minutes ago. The best
thing to do in this case is to focus on where the points begin
and end—as if each point were its own lecture—and identify
their relationships later.

*Type 2: The Reader.* This is the prof who spends the whole
time either uncreatively rephrasing or reading verbatim from

the textbook. Though this guarantees a numbing lecture, it can also give some big hints as to what the professor thinks is important (i.e., what he will put on the exam). Bring your textbook to class and follow along; anything the professor emphasizes, repeats, or draws your attention to is a good thing to highlight or otherwise mark in your book.

*Type 3: The Disaster.* Lots of professors don't seem to have a clue as to how the ideas are connected. (Beware! Some professors are really smart and give complicated but relevant lectures that may resemble the Disaster.) Closely related to the Rambler, this one doesn't even know where his own topics begin and end. About the best thing to do in this case is to go back over your notes after class with a different color ink or pencil and try to identify different topical areas. If you want to go further, you can rewrite the notes afterward according to these topics. This is also a really good time to try to get notes from a note taker or teaching assistant (TA), who might have some familiarity with the Disaster and might be able to make some sense out of the lectures.

*Type 4: The Speed Demon.* This is the guy who races through his material in the hopes that putting material out at twice the speed will somehow allow more of his grand body of knowledge to flow into our heads as we eagerly absorb all that he says. Actually, we are just eager to leave. Whether it's because of a processing or memory issue, the Speed Demon is a problem for almost all of us. This is another good place to use the TA or a note taker's notes to supplement your own efforts. If you can get these, still take notes in class but don't get specific at all—no details, just topics. Then use the TA or note taker's notes to fill in the details afterward.

Before a lecture begins, keep in mind the style of your professor and act accordingly.

### *Your Notes, Your Call: The Relevance Scale*

Lecture is hardly black and white; the challenge is to filter through the mix of relevant and irrelevant information that *is* lecture. At one end of the scale are those juicy tidbits of important knowledge that you must have in order to understand and pass the course. On the other end are stories about Aunt Betty's vacation to the Jersey shore and other useless tangents. The difficulty is not telling the difference between these two extremes but rather discerning the value of the information that falls in between the two extremes.

*The Clearly Irrelevant.* Things that qualify as irrelevant include tangents, anecdotes, and points that have already been beaten into the ground. The primary ways to spot these are through the diction of the prof and the structure of the lecture. Watch for the following:

- **Introductory fluff.** Anything that comes at the beginning of lecture *before* the professor introduces the main point for the day.
- **Asides.** Phrases like "as a bit of an aside . . ." or "I digress."
- **Personal life.** Watch for the "I" voice. Anecdotes about friends or relatives most likely indicate useless information. (If you learn anecdotally, however, keep these in mind.)
- **Third or fourth examples.** Any time your prof goes over a point that many times, it probably means it is important, but you probably don't need to write down all the examples either. Remember that profs tend to repeat the concepts that are going to show up on the tests.
- **Gestures and tone.** Some professors use dismissive hand gestures or a slightly sarcastic or tired tone of voice to indicate something that they don't feel is that important.

- **The professor's personal style.** If he usually belabors a point, the ones that he occasionally speeds through are probably not as important. Some profs finish their prepared lecture early and, looking at their watch, a little embarrassed, say, "Oh, well, I guess we have some time left." This usually indicates that anything else that they say is redundant.

*The Clearly Relevant.* The clearly relevant are theories, ideas, and concepts that are pivotal to the class, will be on the exam, and/or can be covered in a paper. To find these, look to the lecture's structure and the professor's language, gestures, and tone.

The structure of the lecture will become clear in the introduction, which contains the key points for the day and the key concepts that most likely will appear in some form on the exam. Look for the "thesis" statement of the lecture, and try to write all of it down. It may look something like: "Today we are going to talk about $x$, $y$ and $z$." Or, "Last night you read about the causes and effects of $x$." The same goes for the end of lecture. A prof with good pacing should have time to recap and conclude.

The conclusion is usually indicated by statements such as "to conclude," "in summary," "to wrap up." Once you hear these words, write down as much as you can. During the lecture, look for anything that is introduced as an important "broad category." Anything that is introduced categorically (pivotal events, concepts, or terms) and is then described in more detail should be written down. These types of ideas become short answer, essay exam questions, or research papers. If you are in a detail-oriented class in the sciences, look for anything that is introduced as a process. Many times a process is described by steps or parts.

The language, tone, and gestures of the professor will tell you much. Any time you hear one of the following phrases or something similar, think to yourself, "This will be on the test":

- "This information is very important."
- "You will see this again."
- "This is primary to our focus."
- "This is pivotal."
- "This is critical to our understanding."
- "This is an overarching principle."

Along with looking at the professor's language, you can also evaluate the tone, gestures, and presentation aids—for example:

- Before or after presenting the info, the prof seems to get excited.
- Before or after presenting the info, the prof's voice seems to stress. There is no system to identify this, but trust your gut. It's like pornography: you know it when you see it.
- The prof writes the information down. One word of caution: if you have a prof who has a tendency to process things by writing them down, he may go to the board to clear his head, not necessarily to give you the answers.
- The prof reads from notes. Profs sometimes turn to their lecture notes to make sure they clearly articulate an important idea, fact, or concept.
- The prof repeats something. If he or she takes the time to go over some information more than once, write it down.
- Dramatic pregnant pauses. These usually indicate something important has been said. Also, these are sometimes followed by the "you better be writing this down" look. In times like those, take the cue, and write the information down.

*The Gray Area.* The next challenge is to navigate the gray space of a lecture. The majority of lecture is a series of details, examples, and transition words. For some people, writing down all the transitions gives a sense of the lecture's flow. For others, it could be a waste of time. The trick is to develop your own personal way to navigate the gray area. Here is a list of different types of phrases that will cue you that certain information has passed you by or is coming. Once you have picked up on the cues, it's your call whether the information stays or goes. Again, the following information comes straight from Paulk (Paulk!) (you have to take the good and the bad in stride).

- **Example words.** Things like *for example* and *to illustrate* indicate that an example is coming. It's good to get down if you need to ground lecture in concrete information, but can be ignored if it is a third or fourth example.
- **Time words.** Things like *before, meanwhile,* and *after* indicate that a relationship is being established.
- **Additional words.** Words like *furthermore, moreover,* and *also* indicate an additional remark. Many times this will simply be redundant, or else it could be an important brainstorm, and it could give you a new way to understand the point in case you didn't get it before. Listen carefully for what comes out, and act accordingly.
- **Cause-and-effect words.** Words like *therefore, if . . . then,* and *as a result* indicate relationships. Record the two things that are being connected, and listen to how they are connected.
- **Contrast words.** *On the other hand, from the other perspective,* and *conversely* tell you that the other side of the story is coming out. Note accordingly.

With the relevance scale in mind, all that we have left to help you navigate the world of notes is some fundamental good habits to get into any time the notes start flying.

### *The Good, the Bad, the Ugly:*
### *Tips for Effective Note Taking*

Here are our parting shots for note taking—some good things to do any time, anywhere, any lecture:

- Put the date, class topic, and your name on the first page of your notes. You can name and date every page if you want to take this to the extreme. If you feel that it is highly likely that your notes will go the way of chaos, date every paper for easy reorganization down the road.
- Start each day with a new sheet of paper. Write on one side of the paper only. Leave space for ideas that you miss. (You can also add them to the blank facing page.)
- Don't skimp on paper. Write big, and leave plenty of space between ideas, topics, and subtopics.
- Don't try to write down every sentence in order. A good rule of thumb is every third sentence.
- Identify questions or things that you do not understand by using color or symbols.
- Get cheap pens and lots of them, and don't worry about losing them.
- Sit in the front row in the middle. Make eye contact with your prof, even if you are just looking through her or him. Profs like it.
- If your class period is long, take reasonable breaks. It's okay to leave if you come back. However, when you do leave, mark the place in your notes where you left off, and when you return, mark the spot where you picked up again. You may even want to note that there is missing information between those two spots.
- Play around with materials like colored pencils, highlighters, sticky notes, flags, and so on. We learn by process, and you just might find something that sticks.

- Try to get to class early, bring food (you can hide it or eat it on your break), and if possible, bring the caffeine.
- If this is applicable (you know who you are, you lucky dogs), make sure you are medded up for lecture. Black Beauty rides again.

That is all for note taking. Thank God. Now for the last stop for the chapter: reviewing your notes.

## SECTION 3: REVIEWING YOUR NOTES

We have heard a thousand times that we have to review our notes to get the most out of them. We tread lightly here. It is true that reviewing notes is a great way to get the most out of class, but it does not have to take all day. In an ideal world, yes, we would spend all afternoon reviewing the lecture and memorizing its rhetorical structure. But college is anything but an ideal world. Here are three easy and time-effective ways to review your notes on your own schedule.

### Review Your Notes on the Way to Class

You can take some steps toward retaining information from lecture and recalling specific detail in the thirty seconds after class and during the short walk over to your next class. Here's how:

- **Date 'em.** When class is over, sit for thirty seconds and go through all your pages and make sure that they are dated. A little date goes a long way.
- **Skim.** Sit for thirty seconds more, and skim the introduction and the conclusion of your notes.

- **Jet and recall.** As you walk to your next class, ask your-self what was the main topic and the main point about that topic from lecture. Try to formulate this in your mind in two sentences. Finally, let your memories of the lecture run through your mind. Whatever sticks is what works. If nothing comes up, try to remember the lecture visually and emotionally: What was the professor wearing? Where were you sitting? How did the lecture make you feel: bored? interested? disengaged? Whatever is the answer is fine; just always try to ask why.

You're now at your next class, or wherever; your notes are dated, you gave some thought to the main point of the lecture in some detail. Not bad for under five minutes. Got more time? We've got more review for you.

### Review Your Notes During a Break

With a little more time, a table, and a pencil, you can in-crease your retention tenfold and ensure you have useful notes when exam period comes around:

- **Create summary sheets.** You can do this any way that tickles your fancy, but it is best simply to turn to the page directly following the notes in question, label it "note summary," and slap a date on it.
- **Critically read the intro and the conclusion.** With more time, jump into the intro and conclusion of your notes, and edit any unclear words. It does not matter if a word is misspelled or hard to read, as long as *you* can read it. Any words that you cannot read, highlight or underline them, and take a guess at what they are. Any word that you can read but that you struggle with, erase or cross out and rewrite. Also, look for gaps or places where you lost time. Identify these gaps with color or your own symbol. Iden-

tify the main topic and main idea by highlighting them. In a well-organized lecture, these may be indicated by language such as "the main point is" or "the topic of the day is." On your summary page write down the main idea and the main point, each in one sentence.

- **Read main points.** Read topics and main points, and repeat the editing that you did for the intro and the conclusion. On your summary sheet, take a guess at how the lecture's broad categories developed or supported the main idea and topic. If the categories are simply other important topics, try to guess how they are related.

### Review Your Notes at the End of the Day

If you have lasted this long, you really are the stud note taker. For all you master students out there, the goal of this review is to understand the primary topic of the lecture, the main point, and how the lecture developed both ideas. Moreover, this level of review will give you readable and usable notes when it comes time for exams or the big paper.

- **Do big-time editorial.** Reread your notes for editorial issues. Take it from the top (you have already done the intro and the conclusion), and run it all the way through. First, change anything you had trouble reading. Look for terms that do not have clear definitions and identify them with a "??" or another appropriate symbol. Look for spaces where you have lost time. These are usually indicated by what seems to be an abrupt shift in content or logic or an abrupt change in the quality of the notes. When it starts to get bad, mark it. Finally, read for flow and where you think the logic of the presentation is breaking down.

- **Reread for category placement.** This is especially relevant if you are using a two-column note system. You're looking for stuff that ended up on the wrong side of the columns. A good rule of thumb is that if you have a category that runs on for more than two pages, there is probably a place where you can break it up. Look carefully in these sections and, try to identify the broad information that could get kicked to the left side for clarity.

- **Summarize the lecture.** On your note summary sheet, state the topic for the day, the main point, and its relation to the class as a whole.
- **Map or outline the lecture.** The form this will take will depend on your particular learning style. We go with a spatial map, where each circle is a broad category and each line a detail. A traditional linear numeric outline, where each broad category is a Roman numeral and each specific is a letter, also works. If you are truly bold, try some digital mapping. "Inspire" is a great program, but it will set you back some cash.

You now have damn good notes, vastly superior to any we have ever taken in our lives. Feel good; go home. We are all done here.

---

### NOTEBOOK RECOVERY: NOT QUITE A 12-STEP PROGRAM

Regardless of how many good habits we put into effect, the loss of a notebook is still a very real and frightening possibility. When an entire semester's worth of work disappears, we know how tempting it is to make the "rational" decision to drop out of school, move to Tijuana, and take up exotic dancing. Put the pasties on hold for a few minutes, and run through the following steps to see if you can find the notes that you have lost.

### STEP 1: BREATHE

Running around campus is not the best way to get the goods back. Instead, take a few minutes and find a quiet place to chill out for a second. You will be able to pull out of this tailspin. However, first you need to lower your blood pressure a little.

### STEP 2: PHONE CALLS AND E-MAILS (THE SHORT LIST)

All of us, especially those of us who lose things a lot, have people in our lives who always seem to be watching our backs. Call them. See if one of them noticed you forgot your notebook and grabbed it for you.

### STEP 3: CHECK THE HIDING PLACES

We all have those places in our lives where things mysteriously keep ending up. Check these places.

### STEP 4: THINK BACK

Do a more hard-core version of "retrace your steps." Actually write on a piece of paper all the places you have been, in order, since you can positively remember having your notebook. Pay particular attention to anomalies in your schedule: high-stimulus environments, rushed moments, or transition spaces.

### STEP 5: PHONE CALLS AND E-MAILS (AGAIN)

If you think you lost a notebook in class, e-mail your entire class. Also, don't just e-mail your professor, but drop a line to the administrative assistant for the department as well. Cafeterias, snack bars, coffee shops, fast food joints, and cafés have managers who are usually more than willing to help you get reunited with your lost stuff if you call.

### STEP 6: THE SEARCH

Time to hit the pavement. The trick with the actual search is to go in order according to your list of where you have been. Bring along paper and pen to leave your name and number with an administrative assistant, custodian, or cafeteria supervisor.

### STEP 7: THE PROFESSOR

Go to your prof and ask for help. Often the professor's personal notes are too minimal to be useful, so ask if he or she could hook you up with the teaching assistant's notes or anonymously with the notes of another student who takes good notes.

### STEP 8: APPEAL TO THE CLASS

Almost every college student at one time or another has lost some notes and had to ask a classmate for help. If the professor is unwilling or unable to do the note-getting legwork for you, approach him or her or the TA at the beginning of class. Ask this person to recommend a student who takes good notes whom you could ask, or to announce that a student needs a copy of a good set of notes.

### STEP 9: OTHER PEOPLE'S PROPERTY

If all else fails, you can stand up in the beginning of class and explain your situation, begging for a complete set of notes. You could also approach a studious-looking member of an attractive gender and in your most pathetic voice ask for help. Trust us, the last one, although difficult, is worth it, notes or no notes.

SUMMARY

We know you have taken notes on this chapter, so an in-depth conclusion is not necessary. Remember there will be an exam on taking notes in Chapter 9, "Beating the Exam Game." Just kidding. We're happy if you haven't wiped your ass with this chapter yet, much less are reading right now. Anyway, this would not be a hard chapter to take notes on because the bottom line is that there is no one way to take notes. Notes are a personal tool to retain information. They are your tool for your mind. End of story, end of chapter, and now onward with our quest for academic success, to dominating discussion.

# 5: Dominate Discussion

## TALK, GET BETTER GRADES, LEARN, BE SWEET

Need convincing that participating actively in classroom discussion is a big deal? Look no further than that little thing calculated at the end of every semester called your GPA. Many professors count performance in discussion anywhere between 10 and 20 percent of your final grade. That means doing well in discussion can jump a final grade in any class from a half- to a full-letter grade. A B goes to a B+ without doing any extra work. Enough said.

Knowing that you can get better grades simply by talking in class is reason enough to stop right here, find the nearest discussion section, and jump in with gusto, like the Roman emperor Caligula. But hold your Trojans for just a section; discussion gets even better. In-class discussions are places for the budding pragmatist inside all of us, and also learning opportunities that embrace alternative ways to get information. Discussion requires us to engage with the material in a multisensory way, through interpersonal communication, verbal communication, and visual supplements. This type of environment requires verbal processing, a powerful way to learn for anyone. It is also an environment that rewards creative thinking. In discussion you explicate information and answer questions, and you also have the opportunity to make creative connections with information from class notes, lectures, readings, and personal experience.

Too many professors, however, assume that discussion is natural and that any marginally intelligent kid who has done some work should be able to participate in a meaningful and appropriate way. As a result, the only tools we have at our disposal are essentially empty instructions like, "Be a good student, do your reading, and ask articulate questions." In reality, in-class discussion section is simply an academic task, and where there is a task, there is a way. With the right tools, you can take discussion further as both an environment for learning and a way to boost the GPA.

In this chapter we explore concrete tools to participate in discussion. In Section 1, we explore the expectations of the environment and look at four templates for questions and responses that can be used any time with little effort. In Section 2, we turn to the reality of discussion and look at three ways to participate without having done any preparation at all (and we mean *no* preparation). And last, in Section 3, we look at how to prepare effectively for discussion and give you some good habits to get into while you are in the heat of the fray.

## SECTION 1: BLAH, BLAH, BLAH

Discussion may seem intimidating, but it is a very simple environment with very simple goals. It is not an exercise in oration: you do not have to come in with flowcharts and speaking notes, have all the answers, and argue like a Boston lawyer. It is simply about raising your voice and putting in your two cents. Professors make a mental note (sometimes, but rarely, they actually write down who participates) concerning whether a student was engaged and active in the discussion. There are so many students and spoken work is so difficult to process on the fly that it is impossible for the professor to evaluate the true merits of what you are saying while you are saying it. He or she does not have time to break down the argument structure and at best is looking for some key words that relate to the class and the topic. If you talk, you get counted, and you are doing a good job.

To engage more effectively in discussion, grab any of the following four templates. They will help whether you're a master debater, or whether your mouth and nerves take over your voice. You can use these in any situation—if you are walking into class having done no reading or if you are ready to take your class by storm.

### *Template 1: The Active Question*

The active question is an age-old art form that comes straight from the professors themselves. The theory behind the active question is simple. Better than your average questions, the active question integrates a statement of knowledge right before the question part, showing you thought critically about the information in question. Use this at any time, all the time, and get big points. Here's how:

1. **Identify.** The first step is to pick out a subject to ask a question about. This can be in your reading, on the way to class, or in the heat of discussion. Nothing is off limits: terms, theories, concepts, whatever.

2. **Break it down.** Once you have identified that gem of a question, break it down into what you understand and what you do not understand about the topic at hand. Let's say you were reading about tantric sex. You understood the point of longevity but did not understand the first step toward achieving it (ask Sting).

3. **Structure it.** Once you have identified what you understand and what is confusing you, use this structure: "I understand $x$, but I do not understand $y$"—for example, "I understand that the point of longevity in tantric sex is to give pleasure to my partner, but I have no idea how to start that process."

With that done, you have asked an active question. You have thereby engaged with the class, showed the prof that you are an active learner, and probably facilitated your peers' and your own learning. Job well done.

### Template 2: The Ambiguously Relevant Question (ARQ)

This is a powerful tool that students across the country use. Although the ARQ does not require any preparation or background knowledge, asking it indicates a willingness to learn and ultimately to focus discussion on relevant information that benefits the whole class. The ARQ is a question that focuses on a particular core element of any reading or discussion. The key to it is to know what to ask about. When drawing race cars or horses in your notebook isn't cutting it anymore, try asking a question in a similar manner about any of the following:

- **A definition.** Asking the prof to define a term used in the class is a legitimate question. Many times you will be doing a favor to others who may be too timid to ask the question. While reading or just hanging out in the class, record any terms, ideas, or concepts that people throw around without defining. When one comes to mind, try, "You know, I was wondering if we could back up for a second and try to get on the same page. Are we settled on working definitions for [insert term] and [insert term]?"
- **Concrete examples.** Asking for examples grounds theory in the concrete and can give you a focus for reading or reviewing. Try, "I feel as though I have a grasp on the concept, but I had a hard time recalling where [insert term] was in the reading. Could we find a specific page that can stand as an example?"
- **Relevance.** This attempts to draw a connection between something that you wrote down and the broader themes

of the class. Try, "I was wondering where else in the class or in our other readings [insert term] comes up and how it is related to the class as a whole."

- **Relationships.** Identifying relationships is a high level of critical thinking. Ask this question, and you will get the "good question" nod from the prof. With a term, a concept, or two events, try, "I was wondering how [insert terms] was related to [insert term]."

Use the ARQ often and with no shame. The more questions you ask, the more everyone learns. That is a good thing.

### *Template 3: The Anecdotes*

Let us tell you a little story about anecdotes. Everyone uses them all the time: the well read, the not so well read, and guess who else? the professor (how many stories about Aunt Betty's trip to the Jersey shore have you labored through during lecture?)! An anecdote is a personal story that for whatever reason springs to mind in the middle of some academic discussion. Although some may give anecdotes a bad rap, we love them. They spice up a dry academic discussion and are also a legitimate and powerful tool for learning. When you relate information to life, you ground dry academic theory in reality and step toward a richer and more complex understanding of any concept (an alternative learning style called "pragmatic personal learning"; they are all over the place). However, an anecdote used poorly is not a pleasant thing. (How many times have you labored through lecture listening to a story about Aunt Betty? You get the point.) Following are some fundamentals to help you use your life as text (a good thing for art and postmodern literature classes):

- **Think first, talk in a second.** The key to an effective story is critical thought wrapped up and phrased actively. Try not to use your story as filler or just for the sake of hearing yourself talk. Give some thought as to why the story is relevant to the rest of the class and how the content relates to the material being discussed. Articulate in your mind why you are telling your story. Nothing is off limits. It is totally cool if your story is an example of what is being discussed; just articulate it.
- **Don't jump the gun.** Timing is key with a story. The best time to use it is either when the discussion is broad and not too specific or when others are playing the anecdote game. The latter is the most opportune. Do not use an anecdote (unless it is really specific) in the middle of a heated technical discussion. If your class is talking about the breakdown of hydrogen, this is not the time to talk about the time when you were at a Grateful Dead concert and passed out from a nitrous oxide balloon.
- **Keep it short.** Short and sweet is the key to the anecdote. No one wants to listen to a family history.
- **Phrase it actively.** This is the key. Much like an active question, an anecdote is more effective when you specifically state its relevance to the class. Try a very simple form. Paraphrase what is being talked about in your own words, relate your story to the topic, tell your story, and conclude by relating it again.
- **Keep it to one or two a class maximum.** The anecdote is powerful but loses its luster after a while. Try to use it only once or twice a class, and space out the anecdotes.

That's our story about anecdotes, and we are sticking to it. Use them with pride; you're learning better, and so is everyone else.

### *Template 4: The Art of the Three-Sentence Response (TSR)*

The three-sentence response is the big boy of the bunch. It is the most intellectually advanced of the templates and requires a level of preparation (reading), but it gets results. There are absolutely no stigmas around this one. Drop one in class, and you will look and sound like a regular blue-blooded debater. A three-sentence response draws on three levels of critical thinking: paraphrasing, asserting, and questioning. It all sounds damn good and provides you with a very clear structure for all responses. Use this any time, all the time, and blow your peers out of the water. Here is how:

1. **Wait for the kill.** The key with TSR is to wait for a comment by a peer or the prof that you either disagree with or have something to add to. When that happens, take a moment to clarify your thoughts on the subject and then jump in with a hand raised high.

2. **Summarize.** Summarize what your peer or professor said. It is good to use the "I" voice so you do not piss anyone off—for example, "I heard you say that Caligula had orgies with pigs." This shows you are listening, reflects back to your peer what he or she said, and clarifies the statement for the rest of the class in case anyone missed it.

3. **Assert and support.** On the heels of your paraphrasing, make your assertion using a transition word like *however,* *although,* or *nevertheless,* and then follow it up with your reasons for thinking differently. Your evidence can be from a text, an opinion, whatever, but just state it—for example, "I heard you say that Caligula had orgies with pigs. However, I feel that he not only liked pigs but platypuses as well. Let's turn to page 203."

4. **Question.** Pose a question, any question. Ask people if they agree or disagree. If you are bold and feeling confident,

ask the class a more critical question, pushing their thinking. For example, after asserting your point, try, "How does the class think Caligula's fetishism affected Roman sexuality?" No question is off limits here. Be bold.

Keep the TSR in mind any time the class turns to discussion. It is a good model for almost any type of response that gets results and will boost your participation grade.

The TSR concludes our templates for questioning and asserting. To recap: Discussion section is not brain surgery; all the professor is looking for is to make a mental note of your participation. If you get nervous, talk too much, or are simply looking to improve your ability to communicate, grab one of the four templates. They can be used whether or not you have done any reading to up your grade and your learning curve.

## Section 2: The Art of Going to Class Unprepared

In an ideal world, we would prepare flowcharts and speaking notes—in short, do some prep for discussion (we'll get to this in a moment). This, however, is not the reality. The discussion section of class often falls to the bottom of the priority list as does the reading, and more often than not we roll into discussion with little reading done or none at all. Faced with this situation, you think you have a few options: blow off class, go to class but sit in the back quietly, or shoot your mouth off in an unproductive way. The correct answer is: None of the above. In fact, you can take some steps toward asserting yourself in discussion without doing any preparation at all. Unprepared, prepared—for right now, who cares? Learn the art of going to discussion unprepared, go to class, talk, learn, be sweet. It is a

healthy experience to go to class without doing the work and
kick ass.

### *The Art of Talking About What Other People
Are Talking About*

This section is about what to do on days when you don't
even remember your name. We're talking no textbook, no
notebook, no syllabus, definitely no reading or studying—
you're lucky if you have your clothes on and you're sober.
Some folks would tell you to stay home, but they are the weak
of spirit. We say go to class, be proud, but understand your
limitations. All you are really going to be able to do is ask some
ambiguously relevant questions and talk one or two times.
Here is what to do:

1. **Get set up early.** Try your best to show up to class on time
and sit in the front row, giving off the appearance of being both
engaged and prepared. Also, discreetly borrow a pen or a pencil and something to write on. Date the top and divide it into
three columns, and mark them: Terms, Readings/Evidence,
Other Statements.

2. **Listen for terms and readings.** For the first ten minutes,
chill out and write down any terms or readings that are men-
tioned in the appropriate column. Try to identify which terms
reference which readings. When your list starts to grow and
you're feeling confident, ask an ambiguously relevant question
(AQR) about one or two of the terms. Phrase it however you
like, but all you are really doing is asking for their definition—
something like, "Can we get on the same page about what $x$
and $y$ mean?" works best. One down.

3. **Listen to peers.** With this question asked, chill out even
more. You have one down. If you are feeling ambitious, focus
your notes on your classmates' statements. Try to break down

interesting statements to their main point; if possible, extract a coherent thesis. When one does catch your attention, for whatever reason, try a really ambiguous three-sentence response—for example: "What I hear you saying is [insert the classmate's statement]. You know, I can really relate to that idea. I saw it in my own life when . . . [insert personal anecdote]. So do you think I am on target about [insert main point]?"

With the three-sentence response out there, you can now kick back in class anxiety free. You've already talked more than 50 percent of the class. If you want to do a little bit more, all you have to do is try to remember your notebook next time.

### The Art of Talking About Your Notebook

Although we can give off the general appearance of being engaged in class without having anything at all with us, when we bring our notebook with us we can go a bit further. So if you find yourself in class with nothing to arm your intellect except your notebook, relax and follow the following steps:

1. **Scan the syllabus.** Review your syllabus looking for the topic of the day's discussion and the name or subject of the text you were supposed to have read. As soon as conversation starts, ask the class to clarify the topic of conversation for the day. Try something like, "Before we get too far into conversation, I was wondering if we could all get on the same page as to the definition of [insert day's topic]."

2. **Review notes.** With that question asked, sit back, relax, and thumb through your notes from lecture and other discussions looking for any reference to the topic, reading, or author for the day. (If your notes are no good, go back to talking with-

out anything.) If you hit gold, try a three-sentence response (TSR) about the topic of the day. Summarize generally what the class has been saying about the topic. If the class has not touched on it, say that no one has touched on it. Then in your own words, assert what is said about the topic from your notes. Last, ask people if they agree.

3. **Review notes again.** If you are itching to keep on talking, look over your notes for a day that you remember well, and after reviewing try to isolate its main point. When the conversation seems interesting or someone makes a comment you think is relevant to the day's topic, ask the class about how the two days are related using a TSR. Paraphrase a classmate's main point, assert the main point from a previous lecture or class, and ask how the day's topic relates or differs. Try, "I was wondering how [insert day's topic] is related to [insert previous day's topic from notes]."

For the most part your talking for the day is done. Relax, listen to what other people have to say, and take notes. And next time if you want to participate even more, well, bring your book and we'll tell you how.

### *The Art of Discussing a Book You Haven't Read*

This is the scenario you will find yourself in most often. You're in class, you have your notebook and the required reading for the day, but you have no idea what is behind its flimsy cover. Faced with this scenario, you may be tempted to randomly turn to any page and start reading, hoping that conversation may go in that direction. Resist that temptation for a minute or two. We have some steps you should take first. Add the following steps to reading your notebook (you have probably asked between two and three questions already):

1. **Do a focused skim.** After reviewing your syllabus and notes and asking the appropriate questions, identify two or three main terms or ideas that are floating around the classroom. After you have identified them, review the table of contents of the reading for headings that look similar to the buzz words that are going around. Then skim the chapter or pages where this word or idea is located. Now it's time for a TSR. Summarize the buzzwords. Relate to the text and question.

2. **Contextualize.** Jump ahead or back a chapter from where you located your buzzword. Skim this chapter by reading the introduction (probably the first two paragraphs) and the conclusion (the last two or three). Identify the main point of the chapter or the thesis. With these page numbers marked, make a TSR using your buzzwords. *Summary*: "I understand [insert buzzword]." *Assertion*: "I also understand [author]'s discussion of [the main point of the chapter you just skimmed]." *Relationship*: "How does the class see these two ideas developing or relating?"

3. **Look for specific page references.** When a classmate attempts to identify "evidence," ask for a page reference. Anytime you are given a specific page reference, repeat the above steps and make the appropriate TSR.

Following these steps, you will have engaged with the class material and asked thoughtful questions without opening your book. If you want to get even more done, you could try a little reading and, more important, a little preparation.

SECTION 3: EFFECTIVE PREPARATION AND GOOD HABITS

We have to be straight with you. If you are reading this chapter, looking to figure out how to do full PowerPoint presentations, and get pointers on personal presentation style, you're reading the wrong book. For those things, get a book by some Harvard guys. Efficient prep for discussion is also not brain surgery; just do the reading. This section covers what to read to give you the most ammo in discussion. We then leave you with some simple principles for any discussion class you are in.

---

## THE 60-SECOND NOTE CARD

The 60-second note card is key for effective preparation. It is pretty simple. Set aside a page in the appropriate notebook or grab a 3-by-5-inch index card and label it "Discussion notes." Divide your page or card into four sections and title them: Thesis, Argument Development, Broader Themes, and Abstract Connections. If you want to take this to its extreme, set aside another page for each individual chapter in the text (or sections if the text is an essay or chapter). For each chapter or section, create a heading with the title, and create a section for Main Point, Comments, and Questions. Finally, grab a bunch of highlighters—one for the thesis, terms, and other relevant topics with each section. As you read, take your notes on this little card, bring the card to section, and talk away. All is good.

---

### Discussion Points

Many study skills books say simply do the reading, and you are prepared to talk. But that is only half true. Sometimes we can do a reading, and the class never gets around to what we wanted to talk about, leaving us hanging out to dry, with no talking points, and a night wasted in the library. At other times, we may do the reading and get overwhelmed with information, leaving more confused than when we started and no more prepared to chat come D-Day. The key is to prepare effectively, paying close attention to things that are universally valued in every classroom you will ever enter in college. To do this, you need to get a space to hold your thoughts. While in discussion, if you hit on any of the following (some more than others) you will get big points from the prof and facilitate the other students' learning. Here is what to look for and how to find it:

- **Thesis.** The thesis is the main point of any text. Bringing it up in discussion makes you look good and helps everyone in the class understand the reading a little bit better. Nine times out of ten, the thesis is at the end of the introduction *and* at the beginning of the conclusion. To find the thesis, skim your text over lunch (see Chapter 6, "Less Reading, More A's"). When you find it, hold on to it, page number and all. It is perfect for the first comment of the class, making it clear that you did some serious interacting with the reading. Try, "I was wondering if we could begin by looking at the author's main point. I felt it was [insert the thesis statement off your card]."
- **Broader themes, abstract connections.** With these connections, you attempt to place the book in the context of the class as a whole and integrate it into what you already know. To do this, try to identify how the book is related to the topic for the day, days past, and the course as a whole. To refresh your memory you can reread the syllabus and course description, and skim your notes. There is no right answer to this one; just write what you think. Also let your mind wander, and don't censor yourself. If you think that the book currently assigned is related to a previous class on tantric sex, go with it. Say this stuff whenever you want to. This is the good stuff. Share it with others.
- **Argument structure.** Understanding the argument structure gets you big points with both the gods of learning and the prof. To figure out the argument structure, first think

about the thesis of the book. Next, skim the entire table of contents. See if you can identify the methodology of the text. It is best to use this one after engaging with a discussion of the thesis of the text. The goal here is to make a tentative assertion of how the author structures the argument of the thesis.

- **Specific evidence.** Being able to cite specific evidence is the icing on the cake. To do this, read to the level of reading the introduction and conclusion (see "In the Library over the Weekend" in Section 2 of Chapter 6). However, although this evidence will show that you read the book, the conversation will very rarely give you an opportunity to throw it in. Our recommendation is not to spend too much time obsessing over evidence. If it comes up, great; if not, let it slide.

Keep these four little items in mind as you read, record them when you find them, and you will be set for class. Last on our list are some good habits to implement in any discussion section.

### Parting Shots: Good Habits for Any Chat

All that is left to do is tie up some loose ends by checking out good habits for any discussion section. Last stop:

- **No fear.** Although many of us have a traumatic history with discussion section, realize that it is there to help us learn and improve our grades. If the terror strikes you, try taking some deep breaths, imagine the rest of the class naked, and then grab one of our templates and tell yourself that you are just going to speak one time, and one time only. If you do, then the day has been a success.

- **Up close.** A good rule of thumb is to sit front and center for any class. It shows that you are engaged, it gets you closer to the information, and it makes it hard to slip off mentally to the back of the room.
- **Nonverbal, no problem.** If you are truly nonverbal, hate to talk, cannot talk, whatever, try to be honest with your professor. Go to him or her during office hours, explain what your deal is, and try to work out some accommodations—maybe extra credit assignments or study questions as opposed to participating in the class. Or have the professor give you study questions before discussion that you can answer during class. If you are nervous about being called on randomly, have the teacher make a deal never to do that or to cue you by standing in front of you before you are called on.
- **Be honest.** This does not happen very often in college, but if you get called on to answer a specific question and do not know the answer, be honest. Say, "I am sorry, but I don't seem to know the answer to that one." It is the best way to get out of a potentially embarrassing situation.
- **Fidget and split.** If you are a little on the hyperactive side and have a hard time sitting through discussion, try bringing something in to class to fidget with. A rubber ball or a Koosh ball is totally cool (Dave knits in class). Also, try getting up and going to the bathroom once or twice during discussion. It does not matter if you are going to the bathroom or not; go take a walk, get a drink, whatever. A little break does wonders to reduce the hyperactive energy. For both of these, get some clearance ahead of time with the good old prof.
- **Less is more.** Talking too much is never a good thing. A good rule of thumb is two talks per half-hour. Many of us talk to stay focused, so if you have a hard time monitoring your chatting, try the Fidget and Split. Also, if you talk too

much, tell your prof why, and ask to be called on every third time you raise your hand. Or make a deal that he or she will tell you verbally or nonverbally when you are talking too much. A cue works great for the latter.

That's it for the good habits. Use 'em, talk, and you will be sweet.

SUMMARY

Well, it's that time of the book again (as you will see, if you actually keep reading, we don't like the good old summary all that much), and we have talked your ear off, so we'll get to the point. In-class discussion is a great place to pad the GPA and an even better place to learn by processing verbally, a rare moment in an academy dominated by written work and linear thinkers. So, as with all other good endings, we come full circle: Talk, learn, be sweet.

# 6: Less Reading, More A's

It's the start of the semester. You scan your class syllabi for the amount of reading you'll have to do over the semester: organic chemistry, 500 pages; world history, 1,000 pages; postmodern literature, 500 pages (but it is one long sentence).

If you're anything like us, a haunting image comes from the depth of your academic subconscious, straight from the halls of elementary school. You see it coming, and automatically you tell yourself that you have to read every page of every book assigned: the table of contents, footnotes, bibliographies, flap cover, back cover, what the teacher writes on the board, and the lines of sophomoric poetry written in the bathroom stalls.

We are taught to believe at an early age that our ability to perform in reading is the ultimate measurement of intelligence. Moreover, we are taught that any kid who does not read every book cover to cover is a cheater, lazy, stupid, or a combination of all three (yours truly). So in college we wasted a lot time locked in the library reading and rereading until our eyes bled, believing that the act of reading somehow held the key to good grades and thus good moral hygiene.

What they don't tell you at freshman orientation is that in college, you don't have to do all of the reading to get good grades. Reading a textbook cover to cover, like a form of penance, an academic Hail Mary, is inefficient and simply bad reading. In college 90 percent of our reading is about accessing information. In this context, reading is simply a means to get at information. It is not who we are and does not hold the key to our identities or our intelligence. Getting information, not the process of reading, holds the key to grades.

## THE GOODS

There is no way around the fact that books are the dominant way to get the needed information in school. In this chapter, we set aside cover-to-cover reading and explore reading methods that allow you to access information in the least amount of time, with the least amount of pain, and in the most effective manner possible for your learning style. In Section 1, we turn to some alternative learning styles like verbal processing and intuitive intelligence in order to learn how to read books without opening them. In Section 2, we jump into Ph.D. skimming, a nonlinear skimming method that you can adjust to your personal needs. Finally, in Section 3 we outline specific reading strategies for reading fiction and for hard and soft science texts, and doing a focused skimming.

First, however, we explore two fundamentals that will improve your reading and your grades in no time at all. The first is the concept of personal purpose as your guiding light through any reading you do; the second is the tool of active reading.

### *On Purpose*

Knowing your purpose is the key to effective reading. Identifying your purpose is not a great existential decision, just a decision about what you need from any particular reading, how much you want to get from it. What is underneath purpose is being personally proactive. When you make a call on a reading, you choose the methods that work best for you; ultimately you are in control.

---

### PURPOSE BOX

How close should you read it? A better question is, Why am I reading it in the first place?

| | |
|---|---|
| I love this book; this book is my life. | Read it twice. |
| I need to write about this book. | Read it in the library over the weekend. |
| I need to talk about this book intelligently. | Read it late the night before class. |
| I need to not sound like a fool if asked directly about this book. | Read it over lunch before class. |
| I need to drop the name of this book intelligently once. | Read it on the way to class. |
| This book is suggested reading, and I have better things to do. | Don't read it. Do those better things. |

---

### *Active Reading*

As you skim, talk, or listen, or do whichever version of reading you choose, keep in mind the concept of active reading. This concept comes straight from the pros (at least they are good for something) and includes good habits to get into. As you wade through the sea of words, active reading gets you involved in the reading by integrating some alternative learning styles.

## ACTIVE READING

A whole host of tools is at our disposal for interacting with what we are reading. Together they are known as active reading—they all work to increase comprehension and retention. The time you have and how much information you need to get will guide which and how many of these you will use:

- **Three-color highlighting.** By using different colors to identify main points, supporting details, and terms, color taps right into visual memory.
- **Bookmarks and flagging.** Identifying important textual locations means that you don't have to take up space in your gourd remembering page numbers. (Bringing a textbook covered in flags and full of bookmarks to class is also the surest way to send a message to your prof that you are committed enough to the class to interact with the reading.)
- **Marginal notes.** Questions or comments jotted in the margins next to relevant paragraphs provide visual cues when you go back over the book before finals.
- **Summary writing.** Reiterating and condensing information is time-consuming, but it is the best way to be sure that you understand, can remember, and can apply in writing the information that you have read. (Written summaries are most useful for readings that you know will be the focus of a paper.)
- **Reading notes.** Identifying the progression of arguments helps to commit the thesis to memory and provides a reference for future use. This is also very useful to have if you need to write about a specific reading.

These tactics really do work. They were developed by the most competent professionals out there and then field-tested by us.

## Section 1: Read Without Reading

In this section we explore four alternative avenues to access the information hidden behind the cover of a text without ever opening the book. For these four methods, you need your master student skills in hand: the ability to listen critically, process verbally, and bullshit (the makings of any good student). These methods allow you to supplement any level of reading, boost comprehension, and gain a broad understanding of the text's dominant themes and overall relationship to the course. To keep academic probation at bay, however, we recommend you do one "reading," loosely defined as one of the higher levels of skimming (see Section 2) per week to cover your ass. With that said, here are four ways to get the info out of a text without reading anything under the covers (or enhance the value of what little reading you have done):

### *Read the Syllabus Instead*

The syllabus, an outline of the entire course, is a little gold mine. In it lie the topic and themes of every reading for the entire semester in short, concise sentences. The goal is to tap into that gold mine and use it to learn about a book you have not read or to supplement your reading to boost comprehension. Reading the syllabus will *not* allow you to pass an essay test or write a paper on a book you have not opened. The goal is to place the reading in a larger context and thus infer the reading's topic. Many times all you have to be able to do is relate a book superficially to the theme of the class to get big points in discussion or to nail true-false questions. Furthermore, if you do go on to read the book on any level, your comprehension will be greatly increased by spending two minutes checking out the good old syllabus. With the syllabus in hand and the reading in question, here is what to do:

1. **Read the course description.** All syllabi have a nifty little thing called the course description. Find this, read it carefully, and look for any buzzwords that come up or anything that sounds like jargon. Pay close attention to the type of course you are in (is it a survey course or a seminar on a specific topic?). Last, and most important, look for the theme or topic of the course. Usually there will be a topic statement such as, "This course will be a multimedia survey of the modern representation of the phallus" or something like that. This is the good stuff. Everything you read here—everything—will have something to do with the class.

2. **Read all headings.** Read all the headings for every lecture, and ask yourself how they develop the theme or topic. Are you exploring different arguments, different theories, or different parts of the body in an anatomy class? Write the theme down, or make a mental note. Pay particular attention to the heading for the day that the reading is due. Ask yourself what the day's lecture is about. The reading will have something to do with the topic of the day.

3. **Check out the book.** If you have not done the reading, look at the title of the book for the day. See if any of those buzzwords are there or if the entry point of the class (e.g., historical analysis) is in it. Look to see how the title relates to the day at hand. Take a stab at articulating what the topic of the book is for the day. Ask yourself how that topic relates to previous lectures. Don't stress if your answers are broad and nonspecific. Keep in mind that you have learned much more about this book and the class in less time than it would have taken to throw the book out the window.

4. **Check out yourself.** If you have read the book to any degree and are using the syllabus as a supplemental tool, ask yourself how the book relates to the themes and topics of the class. How is this reading similar or different from those from the previous weeks? How is the book related to the day's lec-

ture? The answers to these questions are big time for talking in class (see Chapter 5, "Dominate Discussion") or chatting with a prof.

### Read Your Class Instead

If you listen hard and ask the right questions in class, you will leave with an understanding of your reading's thesis, topic, relevance to the course, and relevance to the day's lecture. To maximize your ability to read the class, check out Chapter 5, "Dominate Discussion." For now, keep a close eye and ear on the professor, and have some questions in the back of your mind when the class turns to discussion.

*Lecture.* When the prof starts to ramble, here is where to pay close attention:

- **Introduction.** Professors will almost always introduce the reading and tie it to the day's lecture in varying degrees. In order to gauge the importance of the book, pay close attention during the introduction of the reading to words like *pivotal, primary,* and *secondary.* Also, many profs will dismiss or highlight a reading by body language. Watch for dismissive gestures or an excited expression on the professor's face. If you observe the latter, you can pretty much deduce that the book is important. Pay close attention to how much time is spent on a particular reading. A good rule of thumb is that the more time spent, the more important the reading is to the class, the more important the reading is to your grade, and the higher the reading should be on your to-do list.
- **Remarks.** Pay close attention for a statement of topic. You're looking for the prof to say something like, "Today's reading covered . . ." No matter how obvious or trivial the statement is, write that down. Next, listen to how your

prof relates the topic of the book to the lecture for the day. Listen for linking words like *related, similar to,* and *as an example.* Last, try to figure out how the prof relates the day's topic and reading to the course as a whole. This is a little harder to pick out in discussion, but listen for the buzzwords that you identified from the syllabus and any broad theoretical statements. While looking for those, also look for any other readings the prof references. Note what the link is (e.g., are the readings similar or different?). If you have done the other reading, you have just learned something about the book you have not read (or read very little of).

*Class Discussion.* During class discussion, you can learn as much as or more than you would by pulling an all-nighter in the library buried in a book:

- **Responses.** When the class turns to discussion, pay close attention to your teacher's responses to other students. The polished students will try to earn points in class discussion by stating the theme of the reading and relating the theme of the reading to the theme of the course. Listen carefully; they'll get shot down if they're off base and stroked if they're on to something. Write down whatever gets the professor's approval, indicated by a nod, a smile, or some other verbal affirmation. When a student gets shot down, pay close attention to the professor's rebuttal. Many professors will not only tell a student he's wrong, but *why* he's wrong. There is as much gold in that interaction as in the prof's lecture. Again, don't worry about the details. Go right in for the kill, and try to find the topic of the book, the book's main argument, and its relationship to the day's lecture and the course itself.

- **Ambiguous relevant questions.** We explore this ancient art form in much more detail in Chapter 5, but by asking the right question, you can get a lot of information about a book even if you have no idea what you are talking about. In discussion or lecture ask the following: "I found [insert title] very engaging, but I am having a hard time seeing how it relates to [insert the topic of the course, topic for the day's lecture, or past lectures—see syllabus]." Write down the response in detail. You have just learned the essentials about your reading. Feel satisfied that you learned something about the text and took the conversation in a direction that will facilitate everyone's learning.

### Read Other Students Instead

Other students can be walking Cliffs Notes. *A word of caution:* Use this method responsibly; a good way to ruin friendships and take a big step toward being a bad person is to use others. These relationships function best when both parties have done some level of the reading. However, everyone has flaked out on a reading at some point. If you have not done a reading, be direct and ask a friend or a well-read peer if he or she will tell you about the reading. Then home in on the big ones: the topic of the reading, the thesis of the reading, the reading's relationship to the course as a whole, and the day's lecture. For each question and response, try to reflect back to your friend in your own words what he or she said.

At the same time, try to facilitate your friend's learning. Ask him or her challenging questions about how the reading may relate to another reading in the course that you know well. Ask how the reading relates to a theme that you feel confident talking about. The goal is for everyone is to be lifted up in the interaction. That is good learning.

### *Read Your Professor . . . Also*

This is our last stop on reading differently, but we have to come clean. It is a bold and risky endeavor to go to a professor without having done any of the reading and try to bullshit him or her into telling you about the text. If you can pull this off, you do indeed have a great and unique gift and are quite possibly either a reptile or the son of Satan.

The goal of going to the professor is either to get guidance on a reading you have not done or to test your comprehension on a reading you have completed. If you have not done any of the reading, an honest discussion can put the reading in question in a broader context and ultimately teach you something about the book before you even open it. Furthermore, if you've done a little of the reading, a nice chat with the prof can greatly improve comprehension and give you insight into what is important in the text and what can be ignored. Both of these are legitimate and powerful means for learning that save time and get better grades.

*Context.* If you have not done any reading, heading to the prof can be a very productive thing, but only if you are honest with the professor about your intentions and goals. The first step is to give the professor a reason for the discussion. We tell our professors that a discussion before doing a reading is the best way for us to learn because it gives us the context for the reading, which in turn gives us the big picture. We then relate it to our learning process, touching on how directed reading within a given framework relates to our ability to think holistically and then sequentially.

With that in mind, we approach the prof honestly, acknowledging that we have not yet read the book and are looking to place the reading in a larger context. Sitting in front of the prof here are four things to ask about:

- **Framework.** Ask what main points or themes the reading develops and how they fit into the greater scheme of the course. Be prepared to have the prof either look at you strangely (a cue to move on) or speak broadly and euphemistically.
- **Focus.** Ask if there are any specific points, details, arguments, or chapters that deserve your undivided attention. Go in for the kill and get page numbers. This is particularly important if you read like Jon (very, very slowly) or struggle with comprehension. If the prof tells you where to focus, you'll be more likely to retain the important stuff and let the irrelevant details glide by.
- **Entry point.** Ask the professor to relate the reading to a reading or idea that you are familiar with. This will give you a cognitive framework, and a concrete way to compare the reading to something you already know (the first step in learning). Phrase your questions actively—for example, "I know that we explored [insert theme] in [insert the book you have read], and I was wondering how [theme] is relevant in [insert the reading in question]." This type of question shows you have engaged with readings in the past and that your goal is to gain a better understanding, not to cheat.
- **Guiding questions.** Guiding questions are powerful tools to increase comprehension and reduce wasted time. Ask your professor to give you some questions you should think about as you read. Five is a good number. These five little questions are golden. If you go on to do the reading and answer the questions, your comprehension will skyrocket; and if you do not do the reading, think about these questions backwards. Whatever the prof asked you must be covered in the text, and, thus, you know what the professor thinks are important points and can make an educated guess at what the text covers broadly.

*Testing Comprehension.* The most powerful way to engage with your professor is as a supplement to the reading you have done. Going in and chatting with a prof allows you to engage verbally with the reading (good for all those verbal processors out there) and check your comprehension with the ultimate sounding board, the teacher. Also, going into office hours to talk about reading is something very few students do. Professors love it; it makes you stand out. In reality, if you are this far, you are pretty much just having a conversation. Here are two things to think about that will make your conversation as productive as possible:

- **Make assertions.** If you are going in to the prof, do so with confidence. The point of this conversation is to push your level of understanding. With no fear at all, make some assertions. Assert what you think the theme of the reading was, the thesis, what was emphasized, and the reading's relevance to the course as a whole and any other reading you have done. Throughout this conversation, listen to the professor's responses, ask for clarification, and note accordingly. Not only will you get big points in the professor's book, but you will learn far more about the reading and the course than if you read the book cover to cover twice.

- **Ask for questions.** Ask the professor to drill you with some questions about the reading. Although this may be slightly more intimidating than making assertions, the benefits are great. You'll be forced to interact with the reading, which is a huge step in the learning process. Your professor's questions will also let you in on what is important to him or her and help you gauge how well you know that material.

You now have learned about reading without ever opening a book (or at reading very little of it). Now it is time to address the moments when we have to dive past the book jackets and into the sea of words. For this endeavor, we have a superior tool to guide us straight from the highest levels of the academy: Ph.D. skimming.

---

## WHAT TO DO WHEN YOU'RE SCREWED

We all fall way behind at some point in our academic career. If you are way behind in your reading, here are some things you can do that have worked for us:

1. **Don't split.** Sticking it out can mean the difference between a rough time and an utter failure.

2. **Evaluate.** Write out a list of everything you should have done.

3. **Reevaluate.** Using class notes, classmates, the professor (yes, the prof), or even the kid next door, get feedback on ways to cut the ideal down to a reasonable expectation given the time that you have.

4. **48 hours = extension.** Ask for an extension, but *not* at the last minute—it usually doesn't work and really rubs the professor the wrong way.

5. **Focus your energy.** College isn't a single course. Make a realistic appraisal of what needs to get done and what you can let slide.

6. **Nothing is the end of the world.** Nothing is the end of the world.

7. **Do the next right thing.** When you get behind, nothing breaks you out of a downward spiral like acting. Pick the next reading on your plate, and skim it, or go to your prof and talk about it. The bottom line is to be proactive. The skills in the Active Reading box will give you the tools to grab a reading and do something with it.

---

## SECTION 2: PH.D. SKIMMING

The cold reality is that much of the valuable information relevant to our intellectual, personal, and academic development is locked within the covers of books in the code of written language. The question is how to unlock this code in the most efficient way to save time and energy and get the best grades possible.

Before we jump right in, we have to put this system in a little context. In our lives, the only method we were ever given to read texts came straight from the depths of the reading myth, developed by some moralistic first-grade teacher and implemented by dirty old bastards across the country. Cover to cover was the only way to go, and if we could not do it that way, we were bad boys. But this type of reading addresses neither the reality of school nor the structure of most academic textbooks. The vast majority of academic textbooks and academic articles are not structured in a linear manner. Information does not progress A, B, C. In fact, the majority of textbooks are cyclical and tell you what they are going to tell you, tell you what they said they would, and then tell you again what they told you. That means that the argument is presented three times, and all we have to do is read it once.

The cover-to-cover approach also ignores the reality of college reading: too much reading for anyone to possibly do. So we need strategies that allow us to meet the everyday situations we face. Sometimes all we have time to do is read a book on the way to class. Traditional reading methods do not give us that option.

What you have in front of you now is our solution that comes straight from the trenches: a nonlinear reading method that addresses the day-to-day reading realities. It is important to note that this system is for traditional nonfiction academic textbooks, articles, or essays. For hard science and fiction, skip down to Section 3.

In Ph.D. skimming, your purpose (see the Purpose Box) guides how deep you have to read. Sometimes you don't have enough time, so the key is to spend that time as efficiently as possible. This means that you'll get something out of a book even if you have only the time it takes to walk to class.

Before we jump in, let's take a second to get into the right mind-set. This is the perfect time to apply active reading skills to improve comprehension and bring into play some of the alternative learning styles to spice up the logical and linear task called reading. If you are the type to take reading notes—good for some, bad for others—then check out our method. It breaks the rules a little but is very effective for visual learners. Reading notes don't have to be ordinary in order to work. Grab a handful of colored pens, map out the reading, and connect the ideas in a way that makes sense to you.

Finally, see if your book has summary sections. If you are reading a book with a summary section, don't worry about skimming; it is time to summarize.

With that stuff out of the way, it is time for Ph.D. skimming. Less reading, more A's is our goal. This is how.

### *On the Way to Class*

This is the broadest level of skimming and can give you a rough understanding of the book's topic and the author's angle. Many times this is enough to give a context to lecture and to assert yourself in discussion (see Chapter 5). *ETA:* Under 5 minutes.

- Read the title.
- Read the chapter titles in the table of contents. If the assignment is to read one essay or one chapter, then read the section titles that appear for it in the table of contents.
- Summarize the book's topic out loud in one sentence.

- Remind yourself of the topic of the class (See "Read the Syllabus Instead," page 135).
- Remind yourself of this week's lecture topic (see "Read the Syllabus Instead").
- Take stab at why you were assigned this book.

### Over Lunch Before Class

This is the second layer of skimming and will give you a good understanding of the author's thesis and a tentative idea of how it is developed throughout the work. The thesis is the big one. It holds the key to understanding the text and its function in the class, and you should drop it at any time possible into a class discussion or in conversation with the professor. *ETA:* 20 minutes.

In addition to the tasks in "On the Way to Class," add the following:

- Read the introduction and conclusion of chapters, paying particular attention to the last two paragraphs of the introduction and the first two paragraphs of the conclusion.
- Identify the main point that they have in common.
- Using a yellow highlighter, underline the main point and bookmark or flag the page. This is the thesis.
- Restate this thesis in one sentence.
- Read the entire table of contents.
- Make a guess at how the chapters work to develop the thesis.

If the assignment is to read a single essay or chapter, try the following steps:

- Read the introduction and conclusion of the essay or chapter. If they are not identified by name in a subhead, these are the first and last few paragraphs of the text.

- Identify, highlight, flag, and restate the main point (i.e., the thesis; see above).
- Read any section titles, usually indicated by boldface, centering, or line breaks.
- Read the first and last two paragraphs of each section.
- Make a guess at how the sections work to develop the thesis.

### The Night Before Class

At this point we are really not talking about skimming but good old-fashioned reading. This level gives you a very good understanding of a text's organization and gives you enough information to outline a paper, mention the book in an essay exam, or eliminate choices from a multiple choice test. *ETA:* An hour plus.

To "Over Lunch Before Class," add the following:

- Read the introduction and summary of each chapter— usually the first and last two paragraphs.
- Write questions and comments in the chapter margins and a summary of the main point for each chapter in one sentence.
- Identify how these chapters develop the thesis of the book.
- Look at any charts or diagrams.
- Make a guess at what details support the thesis of the chapters.

If you are reading a single essay or chapter:

- Read the first two and last sentence of every paragraph.
- Ask how these support the thesis of the essay.

### *In the Library over the Weekend*

If you're in the library over the weekend, you are no longer just reading. With this method, you are engaging with the text to a level of mastery that will surpass the vast majority of your peers. With this level of skimming you are set to destroy discussion, take an exam, or write an A paper. *ETA:* Three hours plus.

To "The Night Before Class," add the following:

- Take written notes concerning the themes and arguments as you read.
- Read the first two and last sentence of every paragraph.
- Identify the topic of each paragraph.
- Ask how each paragraph supports the thesis of the chapter.

If you are reading a single essay or chapter:

- Read the entire essay or chapter.

### SECTION 3: READING EVERYTHING ELSE

As the heading implies, we are on the home stretch, and all that remains is to look at some specific specialized reading methods for types of reading that may not be totally covered in the first two sections. What follows are three specialized reading approaches: the focused skim, reading like Einstein (especially for chemistry majors), and fast fiction.

One last word: Keep in mind that these specialized reading methods are not designed to stand on their own. To maximize their effectiveness, use them in tandem with the methods outlined in Sections 1 and 2. With that said, come on down to the art of the focused skim.

## *The Art of the Focused Skim*

The art of the focused skim is a long-practiced tradition by students who blow off reading, get great grades, and learn more than anyone else. We used to hate these people, but now we know their secret.

The goal of this method is to get very specific types of information from a large reading (that you have or have not done; who cares?) in a very short amount of time. This skill is key for cramming for an exam, researching for papers, and for straight up dominating discussion. It works for any type of reading with the exception of fiction, and all you need in front of you is the reading in question. *ETA*: 5 to 15 minutes, depending on the amount and type of information you are looking for.

1. **Clarify what you are looking for.** The key to good focused skimming is to articulate clearly in your own mind what you are searching for. Get as specific as possible. For example, if you start out looking for sex, try to articulate what exactly you're searching for. Are you looking for sexual positions? The history of S&M? Roman orgies? Or are you looking for the obvious and commonly known fact that Irish men are vastly superior to the average? Regardless, try to focus your search, and be as specific as possible. It will make life much easier.

2. **Think about context.** Think about how this information might be situated in the text. Think about what type of information it is: a term? date? event? theory? Each of these has its own markings inside the text. Also think about what type of information may surround what you are looking for.

3. **Don't read yet!** Don't jump right into the search head first. Take a minute. Alternative sources are a perfect way to

get around the time-consuming act of reading. Go to your syllabus, and see if you can home in on a day where what you are looking for was discussed or addressed in class. If so, go to your notes for that day and scan for your cues. If you find gold, see if you can stop right there. Going to the syllabus is also useful if you are unsure what text to look in. Repeat: Note the readings that were assigned for the lecture. After the syllabus and note search, drop an e-mail to your prof or a peer. Explain what you are looking for, and ask for pointers in the right direction. One word of caution: This works best if what you are looking for is a broad theme, not a specific term or process. If you get that guidance, skip on down to step 5, Dive in.

4. **Scan the text.** If you get no love from the prof, approach the text at hand from broad to specific. The goal is to get a list of possible chapters, sections, and, ideally, pages where your info may lie. Remind yourself of what you are looking for, and skim the table of contents looking for any references. If you hit gold, don't jump in, but record the relevant pages. If your text has chapter summaries, skip to the end of chapters and read the summary. Decide whether the chapter really contains what you are looking for and keep or delete the chapter accordingly. Next look for specific page numbers by reviewing the index of your text. Scan appropriately, and record any page numbers. If you are looking for a specific term, turn to the glossary of the text, and see if you hit the jackpot. With this list in hand, it is time to dive in.

5. **Dive in.** The goal now is to get the goods and nothing else. With no shame at all, ignore any text that does not meet your needs. All you are reading for are the cues we identified above. Nevertheless, there are some markers and rules of thumb. If you are looking for a broad concept or theory, read the introduction to the chapter and the conclusion. It will most likely be there. Pay attention to all headings, breaks, and section ti-

tles. If you are looking for a term or literal detail, pay close attention to any words in boldface or italic type.

### Reading Like Einstein: The Problem Solution Approach

To let you in on a little historical joke, Einstein did not read all that well. He had what is known in the business as dyslexia.

This method, for all of you out there whose passions are the periodic table and the theory of relativity, takes a somewhat novel approach to reading for soft or hard sciences. It revolves around what is a seemingly obvious but often ignored fact: almost all hard and soft sciences give practice questions; these are little gems of knowledge and, ultimately, reading guides. These questions tell you where to focus your reading attention, what to ignore, and what gets your undivided attention. This method is simple: Review your study questions before you read a word of your text, break these questions down to their smallest parts, figure out what they are testing or forcing you to apply, and then work backward into the text to find the paragraphs and text that you need to read in order to answer the questions. You learn by doing the problems and reading about the solutions.

One warning: This system may not be for everyone. If you prefer to learn your material in the abstract and then apply what you have learned, abort this mission. This is for thinkers who learn by doing, or applying information. Keep in mind that this is modeled as an approach to reading chapters, not entire books, and is dependent on there being review questions for each chapter. Here is how to do it:

1. **Find your questions; break them down.** Before you read a word, find the review questions. Break these questions

down into their smallest parts, and identify what the questions are testing. Go to one question at a time. Remember that this is taking the place of reading, so spend a decent amount of time. Read the directions for the problem very carefully. Break out the handy highlighter, and underline any active word or any word that implies action, such as *define, solve, explain,* and so on. Also, look for any key words—words that are boldface or italicized, or that appear in a list at the end of a chapter. Many times the directions will tell you very explicitly what you have to know to answer the questions. After reading the directions, ask yourself what the question is testing you on and what you need to know to solve it. Focus more on the question itself, and break it down into its smallest parts or steps. For each step, ask yourself what it is testing.

2. **Frame.** With those questions in mind, go back over your syllabus looking for key words and then back over your class notes for the days relevant to the problem at hand. Skim your notes to get a general sense of the subject being tested. If necessary, you can ask your prof or a peer to frame the questions for you.

3. **Limit.** Limit your page search. Again, much like focused skimming, start with the index, look for key words, and record relevant page numbers. Also, look up any terms in the glossary of the text that you are unfamiliar with. Then turn to the table of contents, and skim it. Paying close attention to the chapter at hand, look at all subdivisions, and try to get a sense of the chapter as a whole. Try to identify its main theme and the way it develops its argument. Read the intro and conclusion of the chapter or the chapter summary to get a broad picture of this chapter.

4. **Scan within a context.** Using the page numbers from the index and the table of contents, jump into the text specifically looking for the key words and concepts from the question. Ignore anything except what is relevant to answering the ques-

tion. Pay close attention to markers such as examples, bold headings, and diagrams. When you find the key words, stop. Go back two paragraphs, and read carefully until you are two paragraphs past your answer. This gives you a broad context to understand the information.

5. **Answer the question and think critically.** Answer the question *after* reading the appropriate section. As you answer, try to identify the highest principle—the main concept—that was tested, and ask yourself how you would apply this principle to another problem. Repeat for each question.

By following these five steps for each review question, you will have covered the vast majority of the content for the class while simultaneously getting your homework done and learning the material cold.

---

### SUMMARIZE THIS

Most textbooks have a clearly laid out summary at the end of every chapter. The summaries are a good place to start even if you are going to read the whole chapter. You can start your reading knowing the thesis, the structure, and some idea of the vocabulary. If you don't have the time to hit the whole book, a careful reading of the chapter summaries lets you get away with a superficial understanding of the whole text in a minimum of time.

---

Our last method addresses the other end of the spectrum, about as unscientific as you can get: good old-fashioned fiction reading.

## *Fast Fiction*

Fast Fiction is our last reading strategy, but we have to come clean with this one. We racked our brains for months trying to deconstruct fiction and come up with some method or approach, but we had to finally face the reality that fiction has no structure, and there are no magical hiding places for us to look under. Fiction has no right answers, and reading fiction is not about getting things right. It is about engaging with the ironies, the complexities, and the beauty of human experience.

We do know firsthand, though, that this medium can be overwhelming: so many ideas, so many tangents that they flood your brain. Here are some fundamental principles to keep in mind while reading this confusing but engaging art form:

- **Remember the fundamentals.** The big fundamentals are characters, plot (actions, events, setting), and theme. As you read, underline every new character, and ask yourself who he or she is. Also, make a chronology of literal events and imagine where they take place. This makes the story real and tangible. Think about the broad themes in the work, and relate them to the chapters and the plot. If you understand these three elements, you can take a test or write a paper about any work of fiction you encounter.
- **Learn some jargon.** There are numerous ins to fiction that are very simple but jargonized: for example, *narrator, tone, point of view, and figurative language.* If you are in a fiction class, you might want to get a book of literary terms. If you understand these and think about them in the fiction you read, you are well on your way.

- **Talk about fiction.** You have to take Jon's word on this one. He can't read well and he can hardly spell his name, but he gets all A's as an English major. This is how he does it: talk, talk, and talk about your fiction reading with everyone—friends, classmates, the professor. Remember that there are no right answers. So go forth without fear.

- **Supplement fiction.** Before you read, think about checking out supplemental sources like Cliffs Notes or literary criticism. Cliffs Notes are perfect to get an understanding of plot and character and a broad idea of the dominant themes in the work. For a more in-depth look at a piece, check out some literary criticism. Use the latter with caution because literary criticism does get a little theoretical and obscure, but it can be useful in establishing a theoretical entry point.

- **Engage.** This is the most important one of them all. When you are into a story, underline, and write ideas in the margins. Reading is about enjoying yourself and learning about the human experience, so go for it.

Keep these principles in mind any time you walk into a fiction class, and you'll sail on through. All done, but wait! We hear a summary calling.

SUMMARY

If you are just joining us, having skimmed intuitively, give yourself a big pat on the skimming back, and skip this chapter. We have little to teach you. The moral of the story, however, is pretty simple. Cover-to-cover reading is not the best way to go about approaching a text. First try bullshitting—what is known in the professional world as "verbal" processing (got to love those pros)—then skimming; then, if you have time, specializing. Following any of these -ings, you'll be set. Read on, because it is now time to write, write, write like mad.

# 7: Writing, Writing, Writing

When we sit down at the computer to write anything—a sentence, a chapter heading, or (God forbid) the occasional paragraph—it feels as if our heads are filling up with lukewarm water. Ideas feel abstracted, and they rush to fill the recesses of our temples, running behind our eyes, dripping down our neck. It's not quite a headache, but more of a dull pain buried in a thick fog—a crossfire of connections, ideas, synaptic misfires, and emotional distress. As we write, the cognitive pain moves throughout our bodies. Our feet fidget, and our bodies contort as we try to force ourselves to focus. We talk to ourselves when we write—a pathetic, angry murmur filled with obscenities and punctuated by the occasional whimper. We develop tics from nerves and lack of sleep, and we live on the edge of obsessive-compulsive behavior, from rubbing our eyebrows raw to picking at our face.

And that is just the beginning. If we do not run away or find ourselves playing computer games, and we stay at the computer long enough to get anything down, we then have to face what we have birthed on the page. Inevitably, our outcomes are deemed unacceptable by the powers that be, and they are painful to live through. Dave's ideas chase each other around in circles, his syntax is baffling, his logic is filled with half-connections and imperfect transitions, and his concepts are lost in the exchange. Jon's documents on Word '95 are so riddled with underlined, misspelled words (about every third word), grammatical mistakes, and incomplete or incoherent sentences that they look like one of those magic pictures—the ones that, when looked at long and hard enough, the chaos and blurred images morph into something beautiful. At least that is Jon's hope as he spends hours on end going back over his mistakes, faxing this chaos to his mom, rewriting, rewriting, and rewriting. And so we labor on and make it through the paper.

There was a time in our lives when we would simply drop the struggle. But beyond the difficulty with the linear medium of writing, beyond the way we were made to feel about our inability to use proper form, there were rare but powerful moments of joy in the act of writing. Although it is difficult to deal with the midnight anxiety attacks, writing is about ideas, about expressing our opinions and experiences. In the end, finishing a paper and expressing a set of complex ideas is a beautiful thing and feels damn good.

## THREE-DIMENSIONAL THOUGHTS, A TWO-DIMENSIONAL MEDIUM, ONE-DIMENSIONAL SCHOOL

Before we could ever arrive at embracing the positive aspects of writing, we had to jump right into that experience, figure out what was going on, and answer the seemingly simple question: Why is writing so hard for us? We used to have an answer: because we were stupid (Jon) and lazy (Dave). But that is simply wrong.

What we have to say probably will not please your elementary school teacher or many of your profs. Tough. Our difficulty with writing, contrary to how we learned to think about it, lies in a reason outside our intelligence and work ethic. What we struggle with is not that we are lazy or stupid, but in fact the opposite. When we write, we are trying to cram emotions, thoughts, ideas, sounds, shapes, the past, the present, and the future into a narrow, logical, and linear box called the written word (no wonder some writers are crazy). In short, our thoughts are three-dimensional, but the medium of writing is at best two-dimensional, drawing primarily on logical and sequential skills. How many times have you thought about writing a paper or a short-answer test and had that choked-up feeling, the ideas flooding to your head? Or how many times have you tried to cram eight ideas into a ten-line run-on sentence? All of the above happens to us every single time we sit down to write a paper, a letter, or even a sentence.

The second reason writing is so difficult is a historical one, going back to elementary school (you could have guessed that one). Those feelings of shame and emotional distress while writing come from the fact that at an early age, we learned that writing is the gatekeeper to intelligence, right up there with reading. As with reading, the assumption is that when given equal instruction, intelligent people will learn to write and unintelligent people won't. However, writing is a confused and dishonest academic discipline. In our childhood, what mattered about writing were not ideas or emotions but first handwriting, then spelling, and then grammatically correct sentences. This experience slowly and systematically taught us to hate writing and took from us the ability to express ourselves. Devastating stuff for a third grader.

As we got older, and especially in college, teachers claimed to view writing as an exercise in both form and content and claimed to value both. But for many teachers, consciously or unconsciously, spelling, grammar, and punctuation continue to act as the gatekeepers of content. When the writing is misspelled or grammatically incorrect, they assume it is devoid of substantive content.

If you are a teacher and take offense at this statement, you should spend some time thinking about whether this is true for you before you write it off. A longitudinal study, accepted now as hard science, shows conclusively that two identical papers, one with nice handwriting and the other with messy handwriting, randomly shuffled into a prof's grading pile, will receive drastically different grades. The paper with nice handwriting will get a full letter grade higher than the exact same paper with poor penmanship. And all we are talking about is poor penmanship—*not* spelling mistakes and *not* grammar mistakes.

In our adult lives, a familiar refrain rings clear: "great ideas, but. . . ." These teachers should put their thinking caps back on. If ideas don't matter, what does? The form? If given enough time, a chimpanzee will write all of Shakespeare's plays. In short, you can teach form, but ideas are priceless.

The question at hand is this: Given these realities, how do we write with less pain, and in less time, and get better grades?

## THE SOLUTION: BIG IDEAS, SMALL STEPS, A WRITING PROCESS

The key to our success has been never to abandon our ideas and to integrate our strengths, such as verbal processing, visual, spatial, and tactical and kinesthetic thinking, into a writing process that lets us think dynamically but write linearly. The key is to have a writing process that breaks down the act of writing into small, manageable steps: a specific, external structure that gives us something to turn to when our ideas start running circles around us. Rather than abandon ship, we can sail through the process step by step.

In this chapter we explore a writing process that has worked for us. Here are some of the central themes running through the chapter:

- **Process, process, process.** This chapter is not the gospel of the writing process. In fact, this chapter is designed so that you will eventually discard it. It is a tool to help you build your own personalized process that meets your needs and goals. Keep that in mind, and look for what works and what sucks, and act accordingly.

- **Get help.** Although many people like to pretend otherwise, everyone gets feedback, asks for comments, or talks through their ideas. We have had help our entire lives (this chapter got faxed to Jon's mom and dad for proofreading, as did the whole book).
- **Individualize.** This is not a one-size-fits-all model. Throughout each step, we incorporate multiple entry points for using different types of skills, for different types of thinkers. Some steps and suggestions may be useless to you, others you may have been doing all along, or you might combine five at once. We've done our best to present a methodical, thorough process that you can break apart and use however works best for you. Take what you need, and leave the rest.

With that out of the way, here we go. This chapter outlines a writing process that starts with the ideas and ends with the writing on the page. You will find four sections: Getting a Topic; Dealing with Sources; Developing a Thesis and an Outline; and Writing, Writing, Writing.

## Section 1: Getting a Topic

Your topic—a theme, a series of themes linked together, a historical event, or something else—is the heart of your paper. A good topic is narrow in focus. It will ultimately lead to setting forth an argument, which then becomes the dreaded thesis. In this section, however, all we are going to do is focus on choosing a topic, so do not stress.

In our process, we spend a significant amount of time here because having a clearly defined topic makes or breaks the rest of the preparation. Also, by spending time developing a topic before you review sources, you save time by not reading useless information—time that can be better spent on the process of formulating a thesis statement.

Before you jump into developing a topic, it is important to know the parameters of your paper. Take a moment to chat with your prof or review the exact assignment to identify what type of paper you are writing. If your topic has been given to you, skip on down to Section 2. Also, knowing the type of paper you are expected to write will give you some guidance on what you need to write about.

---

## CLIFFS NOTES ON PAPERS

While we are all in favor of writing like Joyce when your paper is on *Ulysses* (or even when your paper is on Steinbeck), it is sometimes helpful to have an understanding of what your professor is expecting your paper to look like. Here are some definitions:

- **Theme**—a relatively short paper that is thesis driven and may reach its conclusions from your analysis, the conclusions of the reading, or your personal experience; the primary form of a paper in humanities classes.
- **Critical essay**—a specific type of theme, which argues toward a conclusion based on your opinion and a critical interpretation of the reading.
- **Report**—a fact-based presentation of research, with the format usually given to you.
- **Research paper**—based on research of published material and arguing a thesis on a topic that is either of your own invention or provided to you.
- **Response**—short, usually less formal, reactions to literature or art, most commonly assigned less for evaluation of your level of critical engagement and more to provide a motivation to do the reading and engage the piece.

You also need to do a little shopping (see the Shopping List box). For this section you will need a new notebook that you will use exclusively for the paper at hand.

---

### SHOPPING LIST

This is kind of like shopping for prophylactics: you need to get them before you can do the deed responsibly; buying them gets the blood going and the mind thinking about what you'll be doing later; and it can even take some of the nervousness out of actually using them. Now if there was only some way to deal with the performance anxiety . . .

- **Highlighters and flags.** Buy at least three colors of high-lighters and three colors of tape-flags that match. You'll use these to add color to the process of organizing textual information.
- **A separate notebook section.** Try setting aside a separate space for your paper. (This is a good idea no matter what type of paper you are writing.) This not only allows you to make outlining a more centralized and efficient process, but also works as a "desktop space." This is a place where you can record all the random (i.e., the good stuff) thoughts that you have concerning your paper as you go through this process.
- **Tape recorder.** If you're into the oral stuff, this is a necessity.

---

This section presents three methods for developing a topic: our own minds, our notes, and our syllabus. You can engage with all three of these in whatever order you like or skip them entirely if a topic comes to mind right away. On each step of the way, you will want to record anything that you may want to write about on a new sheet of paper in your notebook. Use whichever is most appropriate for you. Keep in mind: This is *your* paper and *your* topic, and in the end, you should go with your gut.

### Method 1: Prewriting

Prewriting is not for everyone. It is best if you are the type of thinker whose mind works by meandering through different ideas. It is totally cool if you know that you need to write from a place of structure. If you are still with us, your prompt is, "What do I dig in this class?" With one of the following, just let your mind go:

- **Brainstorm.** Write the name of your course, and let yourself go with whatever comes to mind. If you are at a loss, try using your syllabus as a starting point: read the description of the course, the lecture titles, and everything else. If you know that brainstorming does not work for you, skip this.
- **Free-write.** If you find yourself itching to engage with this process by jumping into the writing, try a free-write—writing without stopping for three minutes. Then go back and look for anything that came up that seems to you to be paper worthy. Highlight this, and if necessary, rewrite it while it is fresh in your mind.
- **Spiral free-write.** This one throws a twist onto the straight free-write. Start with one topic and free-write for two minutes. Then pick a new topic from what sounds good in what you produced. Do this a couple of times, and some pretty tight ideas might start to emerge.
- **Talk it out.** Get a tape recorder, or grab a friend, and spend five or ten minutes talking about your course and what you dig. If he or she is a really nice friend, have this person take notes while you talk. Otherwise record the conversation and take notes when you play it back. Now

go back to your brainstorm and review it with a pen in hand. You are looking for anything that came up that has potential as a paper topic.

## Method 2: Reviewing the Syllabus

Going to the syllabus to get a topic is pretty straightforward. First, reread the course description. Remind yourself of the topic for the course or of some of the dominant themes, and record them appropriately. Next, go through your notes from all the lectures, and pay close attention to the headings. Ask yourself how the headings are related to the themes in the course. Anywhere in that exchange is a possible topic: the themes in the course, the headings, or their relationships.

## Method 3: Reviewing Your Notes

Go back through your lecture notes looking for interesting things that you marked over the course of the semester (see Chapter 4, "Taking Notes Further"). When you find one, critically read it and see if a topic is lurking in there somewhere. If you find a potential topic, record it and review the entire day of notes. Also, just think about the possible topic you identified and write down one sentence about it on your sheet. Record the date of the lecture, the title from the syllabus, and the reading for the day.

## Now What?

Now that you have this huge list of possible topics in front of you, it is time to choose a topic (don't fret, this is a good thing) and take a stab at turning your topic into an argument. This will make the rest of the process go more smoothly. If you have your topic in mind, start on your argument. If you have a daunting list in front of you, here are some things to consider in paring it down:

- **Eliminate.** See if you can eliminate any of your topics. Ask yourself: Is this really a topic as defined by the assignment? Does it interest me? Does it have an appropriate focus—neither too narrow nor too broad? Is it a complete, single idea?
- **Combine.** Once you have eliminated topics that don't work, try to combine some of the ones remaining. To combine, think about the relationship between two topics. Is there a broad category that unites or covers both of them? Think about your type of paper. Do you need multiple things to focus on, like for a compare-and-contrast assignment? When you combine, don't worry if the new topic looks nothing like either one.
- **Choose.** Time to go with your gut and choose a topic. The big question is, What do you want to write about? Don't worry about whether it is smart, or good, or anything else. Just pick it, and go full steam ahead.

Now that you have a topic, the task is to figure out what you have to say about it. This is by no means a thesis or an argument, but the outcome will save you time for reviewing. This is possible only if you have some ideas floating around in your head about your topic. So if you are starting from scratch on this one, jump down to Section 2, "Dealing with Sources." If not, do a little more brainstorming to clarify your thinking on the topic. Ask yourself, What do I know about the topic? What has the class said about the topic? What do I have to say about the topic? After the brainstorm, in some formal manner write out what you are planning to argue or explore about your topic. Let that statement be your guide through the remainder of the process, and move on to getting and reviewing your sources.

## SECTION 2: DEALING WITH SOURCES

Sources are key for the vast majority of upper-level writing assignments. If you are lucky and your assignment does not require any sources at all, skip this and move on to Section 3. If you are unsure, go back to that handy review sheet and see if any sources are required. If so, how many, and what are they? If research and review are in your future, you are in the right place.

Too often in our school experience, we thought we had to review every relevant book in the library for a paper. You do not have to review everything under the sun. What you do wind up reviewing will not only satisfy your professor but also, by following this method, help you clarify your thoughts, which is a big step toward developing a thesis.

Our first step is to build a manageable source list and then effectively review it.

### *Screw the Canon: Developing a Short Source List*

Our goal is to build a manageable source list that contains books that are relevant to your paper and will not waste your precious review time. The first step is to review your assignment for the number of required sources, and any sources that are recommended.

First, turn to the required readings listed in your syllabus. Skim these by reading the titles, tables of contents, and thinking critically about their context by looking at what the week's or day's lecture was about. (The same can be done for shorter readings. Critically read the title of the chapter or article, and any section titles or headings.) Ax the sources that are irrelevant to your topic.

With this refined list of sources, skim all of your sources to the level of having a general understanding of their thesis. (For more on this see "Over Lunch Before Class" in Chapter 6.) If the range of your source list is not specified, settle on two to three sources for up to a fifteen-page paper and three to five sources for anything longer.

If your paper does not require research, then your source list is all set and it is time to review. If, however, research is in your future, you need to go do the outside research.

### Gold Digging: Doing Research

If you are reading this section, we truly do feel for you. Nothing can be more overwhelming than a big research paper. All those books, so little time, and so many different directions to go in. And unfortunately, there is not a science for researching. The goal is to get the goods without getting lost in the library or on the Web. Here are some things to keep in mind that will help you navigate the sea of shelves in the library and the endless number of hits on the Web:

- **Love your librarian.** The most useful resource in the library is the resource librarian. He or she is a professional expert in everything, trained to help even the most disheveled college students find what they need. *Helpful hint*: Be friendly and grateful. Librarians are incredibly underappreciated and are usually taken for granted. This means that if you ask nicely and show your appreciation, you have a very powerful ally in your academic corner.
- **Less is more.** No matter what type of resources you are reviewing, when you are looking for information on your topic—the Internet, on-line catalogs, or bound literature guides—the key is to start looking for your topic in the most specific terms possible. Your search for "human reproduction, natural aptitude of ADHD individuals" will inevitably net a more workable number of entries than "sex."

- **Hitting the books, better.** When you have a good selection of materials on a topic or set of topics (especially if the topic is somewhat unfamiliar to you), a good rule of thumb is to start with the least scholarly and proceed toward the most scholarly. This is not a hard and fast rule, just a tactic that allows us to double-check our understanding of a topic generally before we jump into an in-depth analysis.

### Reviewing Your Sources

The goal here is to read only information that is related to the scope of your argument. By focusing your reading, you can further develop your ideas and ensure you have something to say when it is time for the quotes to come flying. Read the mandatory texts first, recommended texts second, and then just pick some of the rest and be done with it.

To review, we use the focused skim (covered in Chapter 6), and have a notebook and some highlighters handy. On the top of a blank page, we rewrite our topic and tentative argument, if possible. Below that, we divide the first page of notes into two columns, one labeled "page numbers," the other labeled "comments." While reading, identify any passages, ideas, and concepts that are important or relevant to your paper using highlighting and underlining. The act of physically interacting with the text can help you remember the material better. Highlight it according to the type of information it is (a category of information or a detail, a theory, or something else). Also, flag the page with a matching color if possible.

When you find something that makes the cut, record the page number on the left side of your notebook. On the right, do the following:

- Record all thoughts that come to your head right off the bat—whatever pops up.

- Ask yourself what the passage is saying on a literal level. Put it in your own words.
- Remind yourself of your argument or topic statement.
- Ask yourself why you underlined that piece of information. How is it similar to or different from your ideas for the paper?
- Ask yourself if it modifies your thinking about your paper. If it does, record how it modifies it in a formal statement. It is okay if your argument has taken a new turn. However, try to keep probing deeper into your topic, as opposed to adopting an entirely new one.

Repeat these steps for every text, and your sources are kicked. Feel good, feel smart, and move on down to the big boys: developing a thesis and an outline.

## SECTION 3: DEVELOPING A THESIS AND AN OUTLINE

The goal of this section is to develop a clear and manageable thesis and an outline. The reason to do this is simple: so you can jump into writing. However, remember that a thesis, more than anything else, will develop organically, and many of the steps occur simultaneously or at a different rate and time than they are presented here. Many times you'll develop a thesis and write the paper, only to realize that the thesis has changed. This is totally cool; go with the flow. View the following as a loose structure to be taken apart according to your personal needs.

### *Thesis, Antithesis, Synthesis*

Your thesis is the main argument of your text. It is your topic plus an assertion or argumentative clause. A good thesis will jump your grade one full letter and give your writing a tight focus. Developing one, however, is maddening and is in fact responsible for two out of five homicides (at least when we are writing). The goal is to break down your thoughts concisely and force yourself to articulate as clearly as possible. If your thesis is hiding in the depth of your subconscious, try the following:

- **Review.** Go back over everything you have read and thought about thus far. Run all your topics through your head, your readings, and your argument statement. Ask yourself if your thinking about your topic has changed or remained the same. If possible, try to make a broad statement that starts with, "My paper is going to be about [insert everything that comes to mind]." Write it down.

- **That one thing.** After going back over the past, try to articulate in your mind what the one thing is you want to communicate in the whole of the paper—the one idea that will run through it all. With that in mind, restate what your paper will be about, and write this down on a new sheet of paper.

- **Break it down.** Once you've got that one thing you want to say, you are on the home stretch. The task now is to break it down. A good thesis consists of a subject (topic) and an assertion (argument). The key is to get both as specific as possible. A good *subject* is one idea or concept. The *assertion* is an argument that is phrased in the active voice. When this is all done, the goal is to have one clearly defined subject and one clearly defined assertion about that subject. Try translating your statement into a subject and an assertion. (The topic becomes the subject and the argument becomes the assertion.) With that done, the task is to ask, "What do I mean?" Keep going with this until you have one idea that is pared down to its most explicit description. Now it's time to go on to the dreaded critical questioning.

- **Ask how and why.** Critical questioning is the key to developing a tight thesis. However, the most difficult thing about critical thinking is that we cannot do it for you. All we can do is tell you where to turn. First, turn to your assertion. If your assertion seems off-point, ask yourself, How is this related to my subject? Put this response in the active voice. Every time you make an assertion ask yourself, How does it do that? Answer and then rewrite. Keep going with this process until you want to kill us.

- **Get help.** The thesis is a perfect place to get a little outside perspective. Have someone sit there, and talk though what you want to write. Have the person ask you questions that force you to explain your argument. If your listener is willing, have him or her record your thoughts for you as you talk them out loud. There is no shame in this at all.

After following these steps, strip away the subject assertion, and ta da! you have got yourself a bonafide thesis and are well on your way to writing an A paper.

The last step before writing, writing, writing is a little thing called an outline. You may be tempted to skip this step, but Simon says, stick around for a moment. Outline time is good time.

---

## OUTLINES FOR OUTLINES

Under the oppressive regime of linear thinkers, the standard Roman outline reigned supreme. However, this tyranny is no longer. There are now as many ways to outline as there are brains, and no one way is better than the other. Just let your cognitive style lead the way. Here are some of the options. Try them all, stick to one, or make a hybrid:

- **Boxes.** This is for all you spatial thinkers out there. On a single sheet of paper, make a big box. The box represents a paragraph. Inside the box, put the content of the paragraph in whatever structural form floats your boat. Once the paragraph is done, connect your box to another with a line. Write in the transition idea and you're set. (This also works great to supplement flash cards for boxes).

- **Linear outline.** I, II, III. Enough said. It's not our favorite, but good for some.
- **Model.** This is the intense one, and it requires a little shopping. The idea is to build your paper, using a model kit (you can pick one up from your local science geek). The goal is to use the model in tandem with a written outline in some form. Each colored ball represents a paragraph, each paragraph is then written out in outline form on a sheet of paper. The benefit is that you get to build your paper, integrating a tactical-kinesthetic memory and learning style.
- **Talk it out.** Oral outlining is for all you verbal processors. Grab a friend, a stranger, or a loved one (if you are bold, all at the same time), and talk out your paper. Have the person take notes. Or use a tape-recorder.
- **Single-page brainstorm.** Much like mapping, write out your paper in the center of the page, and let your mind go.

## Outlines

You may find yourself asking, Why are outlines important? Here's the answer. An outline not only saves us time when we go to write, but by putting our ideas into an outline structure, we jump-start our minds into conceiving of thoughts linearly (i.e., in writing). The outline will be our guide through the midnight terrors, caffeine-induced anxiety attacks, and Ritalin psychosis.

There really is no one right way to outline. The trick is to figure out what structure works best for you, and to be honest with yourself about how detailed you need your outlines to be.

We both used to think we didn't need outlines, and then found ourselves halfway to the county mental hospital at 5 A.M. on the morning that the paper was due. Regardless of what level of outlining you are down with, here are some things to consider doing to make writing all that much easier:

1. **Develop broad categories.** The first step in getting an outline together is to get all your ideas down on how to argue your thesis. To do this, try going back to the good old standby and choose an idea generation tool. First, refresh your memory by reviewing your notes on everything up to this point. Remind yourself of your thesis and ask yourself, What do I need to talk about in order to prove this to someone that knows nothing at all about it? Nothing is off-limits here. You are just trying to move your thinking toward breaking down a general assertion into subarguments. With all these down, go back and try to identify single, discrete ideas. Try to put each brainstorm into an intellectual category. Ask yourself, Is it a single idea? Is there a broader idea that encompasses it? Can I combine a few into a broad category? Can I eliminate some? These broad categories are now the topics of your paragraphs.

2. **Choose a structure.** Choose a structure? Isn't there only one way to outline? If you were reading any other skills book, then, yes, but not for us. Give some thought to how you best think about information; then choose a structure that works best for how you are wired.

3. **Flush out ideas.** Place each paragraph category in its appropriate place in the structure you have chosen. With that down, ask yourself, How is this category related to my thesis? Your answer is the main point of the topic sentence for the paragraph. Through a process of revision, try to get your response down to one sentence. If you find that you are shedding a lot of different ideas as you refine, keep these aside as other possible paragraph ideas. Next, try to support the

connection. Ask yourself, What do I need to say in order to support that connection and what evidence and details do I have to back it up?" This gets bulleted, or placed in random order, or an order of your choosing. Repeat for each main idea.

4. **Talk it out.** If possible, grab someone and spend some time chatting about the outline of your paper. Ask your listener to point out flaws, and have him or her force you to clarify how it is organized. Go one step further and talk about what is going to be in each paragraph. Talking the whole thing out creates a broader context, making life much easier when it comes to writing.

With the outline done, sources reviewed, and a thesis in hand, it is time to take the big leap into writing your paper. If you feel a lump in your throat and are suddenly driven to distraction, it's okay; we have all been there before. Take a moment and know that you are on the home stretch. And then we have some tricks of the trade to bring you on home. It is time to write, write, and write like mad.

SECTION 4: WRITING, WRITING, WRITING

No matter how we spin this section, we all know that there is a huge difference between preparing to write and actually writing. It is hard for us to write. We struggle with getting to the computer, and we struggle to stay there; we struggle with getting our words out, and then we struggle to make them say something coherent. The trick to taking the pain out of writing is to not try and do all of these things at one time. Our goal is to engage with the act of writing as a process of revision and re-creation. In this light, we already have a damn good start. Up until this point, we have been revising and re-creating our ideas, and the structure that will carry these ideas. In many re-spects, although writing is painful, we are on to the busywork of the whole process.

Before you start, it might help to:

- **Disempower the act of writing.** We have already gone through numerous conceptual drafts, and now it is time to do the busywork. Like all other busywork, for people who are concerned with bigger and better things, getting our ideas out is a huge pain in the ass, but it is just busy-work. Keep this in mind.

- **Prepare for "the voice."** One of the most difficult things about writing is that nagging voice in the back of our heads that constantly wants to tell us how bad we are doing. It comes up in different ways for everyone, but the bottom line is that it is paralyzing. Give yourself a second to see how it comes up for you. What does this critic say while you write? Then try to develop a response to this voice. For us, when that little hurt kid comes up, the re-sponse that works best for us is, "Okay, maybe you're right and my writing does suck, but I'm going to revise it later, so let's move on to the next thing, and fix it later."

- **Kill the image of a "perfect kid."** Throughout our lives, we were haunted by the image of the perfect kid who could write a perfect essay in a matter of hours without talking it through, doing wild brainstorming, or faxing a paper to his mom. THESE KIDS DO NOT EXIST. Anyone writ-ing a paper with so little effort isn't exploring very com-plex or challenging ideas. *You*, however, are developing complex ideas, and it takes time and work to get them out, and you're doing a good job.

- **Remind yourself of the power of the process.** You have already developed your ideas and researched the topic. If you get it down in some way or another, remind yourself that you'll go back to it (this is part of the process). If you work through it as a process, you will get at least a B.

There is no way around the fact that for us, writing is a process of revision and re-creating. In this section we look at the act of writing in three parts: getting our words out and on the page, rewriting for content, and the busywork of polishing it off. Here we go.

### Out, Out, Damn Words

Our first step in writing is to get our words on the page in whatever form they may come. Getting our words out is not as straightforward as sitting down to write. One of our first challenges is simply getting to the computer and setting up an environment that is writer friendly. In this section, we explore how to start writing and, once in the swing of things, how to stay writing.

*How to Start Writing.* If you are capable of sitting down at the computer and with a flick of the wrist start writing, you should call us up, because we're looking for another coauthor. If fact, sitting in front of a blank screen, even with a well-developed outline and well-thought-out ideas, is probably one of the most terrifying experiences of the whole writing process. It is common for us at this point to stare at a blank screen for hours, overwhelmed by this massive whole of a paper. If you are like us and blank screen psychosis sets in, check out our cures:

- **Review and rewrite your outline.** Review your outline all the way through. Don't try to fix it or criticize it. Just get the big picture. Then write out a broad version of it using only the topic of each paragraph. Try to have this fit on one page. Keep this page in view as you write.

- **Take some deep breaths.** If you breathe fast enough and apply the appropriate pressure to the head and neck regions, you can make yourself pass out, perhaps becoming eligible for an extension on your paper due to medical reasons. Even if an extension does not ensue, taking deep breaths relaxes you a little and gets oxygen to the cabeza, where all writing originates.
- **Free-write.** Write for a minute nonstop. The idea is to get your mind thinking in terms of sentences and working in two dimensions. For a minute, just write about people in your classes you would have sex with. Then switch it up and write about people you would not have sex with. Once you are done, move right into some form of writing on your paper.
- **Give it a title.** Think broadly about your paper and identify a specific title that explains what you are talking about. With that done, write it out.
- **Rewrite the thesis.** Put this at the top of your page, under your title. *Bold* it to make it stand out in your mind.

*How to Keep Writing.* Ideally, those five suggestions will get you into the swing of writing, but sometimes that swing is gone like last year's dance fad. The next challenge is to keep writing—as fast as you can and in many respects without thinking. You have already done the idea formulation, and it is time to trust the process. Here are some things to help you write on through the night with little pain and big progress:

- **"To-do" list.** We all experience those momentary lapses where we stop writing, take a break, or stare at the screen for a while, only to find that we can't start back up again.

Many times, we click back into the all-or-nothing mode, thinking to ourselves, "I have ten pages more. I'll never finish." To break out of this mode, make a small to-do list, and keep it near your computer. Keep this list small, with no more than two paragraphs on it at a time. Tell yourself that you are just going to write the first item on your list, and then you can take a break, and quit. Many times this will get you back into the writing, and the next thing you know, five paragraphs are done.

- **Rethink writing an introduction.** If you find yourself getting bogged down in the intro of the paper, skip over it and think about going straight to writing a conclusion. Or just use your intro as freewriting. Explore all your ideas for a page or so; then state your thesis verbatim at the end of your freewriting.

- **Turn off spell check and grammar check.** If your computer has any form of automatic spelling or grammar check, turn it off. You can turn it back on when you are done writing. We don't need the computer throwing our mistakes in our face as we get our ideas down. At this point, who cares about mistakes? We'll get to those later.

- **Remind yourself that you are going to rewrite.** When that little voice comes up to tell you that your writing sucks like a new Hoover, tell yourself that maybe the writing is bad, but you are going to rewrite, so things will be fine.

- **Keep moving and talking.** Talk out loud to yourself or move your lips, bounce your foot, or rock your entire body. Keep the tactile and kinesthetic senses engaged with the writing. It helps your brain stoop to the level of written language.

- **Try not to correct.** Just let your writing go. Try as little as possible to erase unless you are sure you will have no idea what you meant when you come back to it. Also, for the first draft, leave in redundant sentences that repeat ideas. These happen a lot and can actually be a plus when rewriting. (They give you options to choose from.) It is okay to write wordy, rambling, and grammatically incorrect sentences at this point. There are some exceptions to this one, especially if you're having difficulty writing on target. If that is you, check out the Relevance Check box.

---

## THE RELEVANCE CHECK

We start writing, get into the flow of the lateral mind, and go go go all night—only to discover that our lateral mind took us in unexpected and unoutlined territory. This is a bad thing only if you think it is. Sometimes the wild mind and wild paper are just what the creative spirit needs. However, you should know that the powers that be very rarely value the wild mind or the wild paper. If you are a roamer in a class that wants to fence you in, try the following to stay on target:

- **Five-sentence checkpoint.** If your mind goes out of control, try imposing a three-sentence checkpoint. That means that every five sentences you stop, remind yourself of your thesis, check relevance, and then move on.
- **Relevance statement.** Another good way to stay on target is to state the relevance of any given paragraph to the paper as a whole. If you do this, bold or italicize this statement to separate it from the text. It is a great way to stay on target.
- **Map.** If your short-term memory keeps you meandering around, try mapping your paper—giving yourself the big picture, where you are going, where you have been, allowing the present to stay on target.

- **Do not write transitions.** If you get hung up on ending and beginning each paragraph, skip it. If you skip them, try leaving a double break, which indicates a transition. In addition, in bold write out TRANSITION, and then in parentheses write some words that come to your mind. These don't have to be complete sentences yet. (There is a whole step in the revising process dedicated to cleaning up transitions.) Sometimes trying to skip the transitions is worse than trying to write them. Try using: "And the next idea is . . ."
- **Parenthetical cite.** Do not get bogged down in citing evidence. If it comes right to your mind, put it in. However, try not to go get the book, and look up the quote. You may find yourself an hour later at the same place. If you get the urge to go get the quote, simply put the book and the type of quote you are looking for in parentheses and then bold it. If you just know that you need some evidence to support a point, but are not sure what that evidence is going to be, just do "    " and move on.
- **Take breaks or switch gears.** Our minds work best when forced to adapt and when refreshed. If you find that nothing is coming out, try switching gears. Brainstorm or doodle for a minute. Also, you can (although we previously said not to do this) go back and do a little rewriting of a past paragraph. This gets you out of the development mode. Or try taking a five-minute break.
- **Do the Next Right Thing** (see box, page 182).

With these hints under your writing belt, you can breeze through the first round of writing and move on down.

### Rewriting for Content

The goal now is to do a full conceptual review of the paper and thematic revision. This step will increase your grade by one letter. Going back to your first draft, however, has the potential to be a traumatic event. It's like going back to the murder scene where your ideas are all tangled on themselves and bloodied with misspelled words and incomplete sentences. Emotionally it is overwhelming just to look at the document. The key is to change your perspective on going back over your writing. Revising writing is like solving a puzzle. All the necessary information is down; you no longer have to make any of it up, and the task at hand is to bring all the pieces together, making it as clear as possible. Like a puzzle, there are specific places that you can go to revise, and things to do there to make the task much easier. We look at reviewing in two ways: reviewing the paper yourself, and getting help from someone else.

---

### THE ART OF THE NEXT RIGHT THING

This is an ancient art straight from an ADHD sect of Buddhist monks, known extensively throughout the world for their propensity to become overwhelmed and then paralyzed. Wherever you are, whatever you are doing, stop, close your eyes, ask the universe to cut you some slack for ten seconds, take ten deep breaths, clear your mind, and open your eyes. Then just do whatever is the first thing to come to mind.

---

First, get some supplies: coffee, four colors of highlighters, and a blank piece of paper. Now assign a color highlighter for each of the following: *thesis, underdeveloped, totally unrelated, confused*. With these in hand, print out a hard copy of your document and go to town.

*Reviewing It Yourself.* Spending some quality time alone with your paper at this point will greatly improve your grade in the end. Follow these steps:

1. **Read the thing over out loud.** Quickly and without trying to revise anything or beating up yourself too much, read over the paper once.

2. **Find your thesis.** On your second read, identify your thesis statement. In an ideal situation, this would be the last sentence of your first paragraph, although not always.

3. **Critically evaluate your thesis.** With the paper in mind, ask yourself if your thesis is still relevant. Does the paper seem to explore other ideas that are not encompassed in the language of the thesis? If so, which ones? Is the language of the thesis too vague? Can you make it more specific?

4. **Evaluate and rewrite topic sentences.** With every new paragraph, identify the topic sentence. Having clear, well-developed topic sentences will greatly clarify your writing and significantly improve your grade. Topic sentences are cues for your reader, and profs dig seeing them. Most topic sentences come at the beginning of a paragraph, and tell the reader what to expect and how the paragraph is related to the broader argument of the paper. However, sometimes in our writing, we find topic sentences buried at the end of our paragraphs, a reversal of sorts. If you run into a paragraph that you are not sure has a topic sentence, complete the following statement: "This paragraph is about [insert topic], and [topic] is relevant to my paper because of [insert your answer]." When this is done, strip off the artificial structure, leaving the topic and its relevance to the paper.

5. **Map the development.** Once you have identified your thesis, write it down on the top of your blank paper. As you move through each paragraph, clearly rewrite the topic sentence of each paragraph as its own box. What you're doing is seeing how the paper fits together.

6. **Highlight the rough spots.** Using those highlighters, identify any statement that is underdeveloped, totally unre-

lated, or confused. After identifying them, go back and give a go at fixing them.

After working through your rough draft on your own, it is time to get help.

*Using Help to Rewrite.* The goal of this step is to use help effectively to improve the intellectual content of your paper. It is not yet time to dive into spelling and grammar. If the idea of getting help here makes you shudder, remind yourself that people who write without getting any help have simplistic ideas. That is not you. Getting help on rewriting is a powerful tool not only for doing tight papers, but also for learning how to become a better writer. To get help, though, it is important to have an understanding of the challenges you face in your own writing.

Take a step back from your writing, and try to develop a reader review sheet consisting of ten critical questions that you want your reader to answer about your paper. Taking this step back will allow you to get some perspective on the writing, and you will be surprised how much you learn in the process.

The key in developing an effective review sheet is to ask critical, active questions and demand specific feedback from your reader. Broad critical comments will do you no good. Your questions should focus on your thesis, the paper's organization, and any specific issues such as the clarity of a main point or tone. To ask critical, active questions, you need to push beyond the obvious, "Is my thesis clear?" and move to, "I tried to argue X. Is it clear? And if not, how can I change it?" Take some time in developing this reader review sheet; it will do you a world of good in the end.

After you have gotten back the comments from your readers

and implemented them, you're on the home stretch. Now to the easy stuff: polishing it all off.

---

## THE WRITER'S REVIEW SHEET

The writer's review sheet has a past reaching back generations deep into the recess of some Irish pub from the Mooney clan. These folk, needless to say, were well known for, among other things, their language processing problems and getting more help on writing than any short mick ever possibly dreamed about. The idea is simple. Before you give a paper to a reader, spend some time (ten minutes, max) to develop a reader's review sheet—a document to guide your reader through your prose. The benefits are many: fame, glory, and better papers, to name just a few. When you give some guidance, your reviewer will do a better job on the paper, and by taking those few extra minutes you can get some critical distance from your work (ultimately leading to a better understanding of the piece and your writing).

Your review sheet can look like anything, but we go with a blank page, stapled to the piece of writing in question. Here are some things to consider:

- **Know your weaknesses.** We've all got them—those little things about writing that give us a huge pain in the ass. When you are rewriting, it is important to jump into these honestly, without any shame, and communicate very clearly with your reader what your weaknesses are. For Jon, many times one word is supposed to stand for ten sentences. In this case, Jon says, "At any point, if you are confused, please say, What are you trying to get at?" Knowing your weaknesses will help the review process sail along even in the muddled waters of midnight prose.

- **State expectations.** When you send your sheet on over, tell your reader exactly what you are looking for—for example, broad thematic criticism, technical criticism, or structural criticism.

- **Ask ten active questions.** This is the core of a review sheet. Go back over your paper, and ask your reader ten critical active questions. Get into your paper, and try not to just say, "Was I clear?" but push it further: "Was I clear about the intersection of points A and B?" Ten is a good number of questions.

- **Restate the thesis.** Tell your reader exactly what you were trying to prove or argue. Forcing yourself to do this helps your reader and clarifies the main point of your work in your mind. A good thing.

With that, you have developed a review sheet. Send it off, and fear no help while writing.

### Busywork

This is the final step. You have worked your ass off, and you have a brilliant paper in front of you. To get the brilliant grade you deserve, however, you have to do the necessary proofreading to appease the narrow mind of professors who believe spelling, grammar, and all that linear stuff are of equal importance with content. That means grammar and spelling time. This is what we do when we're on the home stretch:

Get help! If you can line up some help on this one, you really are done. But we know that getting help is easier said than done. To ease your burden, try your college's writing center or tutoring center. If you give the tutors enough time (you probably have to make an appointment at least a day in advance), it is their job to correct your writing. If you are LD/ADHD, give them a heads up, mostly for your own comfort. Very directly, explain your weakness as a writer—that spelling and grammar are really hard for you. To have this help be most effective, ask them to focus on specific things—for example, spelling and passive voice, and not content.

If that doesn't work, try a friend, your parents (Jon's number one choice), or your partner. When you approach any of these people, level with them. Tell them that you suck at spelling and grammar (or whatever it is for you), and that you need help. If possible, have them make changes right on an electronic copy of the paper; you can send it by e-mail. Also, if you have trouble with spelling, have someone either do it for you or, just as good, have that person in the room or on the phone when you run it through the spell checker. If you are anything like Jon, you will want someone close by to help you navigate the sea of similar words the spell checker brings up for you. (The spell checker tries to help you by giving you a long list of very similar words. Although it is well intentioned, it was not designed by or for a dyslexic person.) When you get a long list that starts to do a little dance, just ask whoever is helping you how to spell the word in question, write it in, and move on.

If you're on your own, here are some things that can make your life easier:

1. **Run spell check.** This is God's gift to dyslexics, but only to a point. For ways to make your spell checker work even better check out the Ten Ways to Make Spell Checker More Effective box.

## TOP TEN WAYS TO MAKE SPELL CHECKING MORE EFFECTIVE

The spell checker is a thing of greatness. But a tool is only as good as its user. Here are the top ten ways to improve your spell checking straight from the mind of the worst speller around, Jon:

1. **Use Auto Correct.** That Bill Gates man keeps them coming. The new Microsoft Word program has the ability to store your commonly misspelled words and correct them automatically. To do so, you have to be in the text and click right on the word in question and choose, Add to Author's Correct.

2. **Get help.** If the words do a little dance in your head, grab someone (Mom, if you're Jon) and have the person chill out while you spell check. If the words all start to look the same, ask your companion how to spell it. *Hint:* Don't choose a dyslexic as your companion.

3. **Use Correct All.** We all have patterns in our misspelled words, and Correct All will pick those up and save you time.

4. **Go broad.** With Word you have the option of going word by word following the red lines. This is not effective. Do the big spell check under Tools first.

5. **Use a dictionary or thesaurus.** The electronic ones are the best. If you don't know if you have the right version of a word (they look the same in some ways), click on the thesaurus or the big D, and they'll tell you.

6. **Take breaks.** Twenty minutes on–ten off is a good template.

7. **Retype.** If you get no options from our buddy the spell checker, go back to the phonetic board and try again.

8. **Spell phonetically.** Your spell checker is hooked on phonics, so go with the sounds, and you should be all right.

9. **Turn the red back on.** If you turned the red lines off, as we suggested, turn them back on when it is spelling time.

10. **Have someone else do it.** This is our favorite of the bunch because it really pisses off the elementary school teacher. We can hear it now: "If you don't correct your spelling, how are you ever going to learn to spell better?" Who cares? If someone in your life is willing to do battle against the phonics, let them. Screw spelling.

2. **Read out loud, and use a finger to follow along.** This will keep you reading what's actually written on the page.

3. **Read backward.** Not a problem for some of us. . . . Reading your paper from the end to the beginning allows you to focus entirely on the language and ignore content. It's a good way to pick up mistakes.

4. **Highlight.** When you run across anything that sounds awkward to you, highlight it. Even if you can't figure out why, there is probably a mistake in there.

5. **Watch for at-risk language.** These are places where you will make many mistakes and have no idea—for example, *who/how* (your guess is as good as ours).

6. **Watch for the passive voice.** Profs love to pick up on it and hold it against us. We are usually plagued by the passive voice, and it hurts our grades. For help identifying and fixing it, check out The Box of Passive Voice.

7. **Check documentation.** If you are writing a paper with quotes and sources, professors will look at how you reference them. (For help in this, check out the Document This box).

## THE BOX OF PASSIVE VOICE

Passive voice plagues our writing like, well, like the plague. Most students struggle with this little bugger. Passive voice is when the subject of the sentence is passive and does not do the action. However, when you know what to look for and what to fix, it is not too hard to cure. And it will help your grade on any paper tremendously. Here is what to do:

- **Look for red flag words.** Although this is not absolute (what is, in a world of subjectivity?), there are some words that are red flags for passive voice: *that, which, should be, was, is, were, have been*. "A man and woman passing by the door *were invited* to join the party." When you see any of those words zoom in and look carefully.
- **Look for passive subjects.** This is the key to passive voice. For example, "The party was assembled by the drunks," is passive. Change to, "The drunkards assembled the party." This is active. The drunks, the subject of the sentence, did the action.
- **Avoid transforming simple verbs.** If you applied for a job, do not say, "You made an application for a job."

8. **Polish it off.** Page numbers, name, class, and a bag of chips—easy stuff that impresses the linear powers that be.

With the busywork out of the way, turn the sucker in, take a nap, or whatever else you do to feel good. You've done a great job.

## DOCUMENT THIS

Documenting your paper is very important. You've worked damn hard, and you want to take the appropriate steps to make sure you are not accused of plagiarism. However, the rules for documentation are far too complex for our feeble memories, so we suggest getting a book of standard documenting projects and giving it a home near your desk. The one we use is Sharon Sorenson, *How to Write Research Papers* (Macmillan).

SUMMARY

It is that time again, and usually for our summaries we defer to our uncanny ability to use sophomoric humor as an alternative to writing anything substantive (it is truly a gift). But not this time. Nope, nope, nope. We have to drive home one key point of this chapter. Writing is one of those activities that is difficult for many people. It is unfortunate that we are made to use writing as a battleground for our intelligence and GPA. For many (definitely for Jon), writing is one of the few accepted avenues to explore a creative and intellectual self. Too often, though, the focus of writing is not on ideas or personal development but on superficial measures, turning an intrinsically empowering act into a moralistic and punitive one. The goal of this chapter was not to tell you how to write but to present a writing process broken down into its smallest parts. That is all we can do, because in the end, what we all want is to write in an authentic way. Finding our voice and crafting a process to express our voice is an empowering experience. So keep coming back to this chapter and use it. It is your tool. When you find a process that works, rip this one right out of the book, because you do not need it any more. Remember to stay with your ideas, and don't ever listen to anyone who tells you that form is the gatekeeper to content. You don't want to hang around those people, because they are not going anywhere far or fun (most likely academia. Oy.). Stay with your ideas, because those are the beautiful things.

# 8: Cram Like a Pro

## PULLING LEVERS: REVIEWING THE ORDINARY WAY

*"If you want to be successful, you had better start to buckle down and study harder!"* If you're anything like us, just reading the title of this chapter in conjunction with that absurd comment makes you feel somewhat incontinent. We certainly know we're running for the Depends every time midterms and finals come rolling around. And with good reason: prepping for exams is a stressful and emotionally loaded situation, not to mention intellectually taxing. So much is caught up in exams; those A's we lust after are the closest things to gold stars.

But in our lives, the only coaching we ever received followed the same absurd logic as "buckle down and study harder." But "study harder" is not very good coaching, is it? What does it mean to "study harder?" Did they mean we should "think harder"? How *exactly* does one think harder? It's a popular directive, at least where we went to school, but no one has yet to figure out what it means. It sounds almost as absurd as the vapid euphemistic directive: "Focus!"

Ironically, regardless of the hours spent "buckling down," no one ever got graded for time spent or for pure effort. We never got any A's for putting in three times as much time and effort as the other kids to read one page from a book, or for the shame and effort it took just to get ourselves to sit down at our desk.

Effort is never valued, only performance. The coaching that was designed to "help" us perform was wrapped up in an idealized and absurd vision of perfect little machine kids with perfect hair and perfect smiles, sitting at a desk with wide-open perfect grins, their papers all in order, perfect handwriting, doing rote algebraic proofs over and over again. But as we all know, there is no "normal" way to learn, although we all suffer the scars of this illusion.

Exams are good for padding the transcript. But they should also be learning opportunities, not lost in the illusion that Dick-and-Jane-type studying is the key to success. We are not Dick and Jane. We think differently, we learn differently, and we should study differently also.

## A DIFFERENT APPROACH

Most study guides advocate reviewing in one consistent way for all the material covered in the class every time an exam comes up. Sorry, guys, not only is this type of review a waste of time, but it ignores the facts that every test is a different project, requiring us to learn different types of information, and every person tested is a different type of learner. The most effective way to review for an exam is not to review everything in a homogeneous way, but to review systematically and methodically, taking into account what this exam is testing and how you learn. This type of review saves time, gets better grades, and is simply a better way to learn.

In this chapter we explore the alternatives to pulling levers. In Section 1, we outline six principles to create an individualized project-based approach for any exam. This approach allows you to review the material in a way that coincides with both the intellectual expectations of the exam (i.e., how you are going to have to use the information) and how your mind learns.

In section 2, with the principles of a project-based review firmly in hand, we look at reviewing for specialized exams. This section covers Cramming Like a Pro, Reviewing for Take-Home and Open-Note Exams, Essay Exams, and Problem Solution Exams.

## SECTION 1: THE INDIVIDUALIZED PROJECT-BASED REVIEW

Too often in our academic careers we approached reviewing for an exam like sinners begging for forgiveness. To humble ourselves, we read our textbooks page by page late into the night. We pored over our notes and created summary sheet after summary sheet. We thought about running the gauntlet, but instead ran through our past experience in our minds and quit to go play a computer game. We thought we were doing the right thing, but all we were doing was pounding a square peg into a round hole.

The key to more effective studying is not working harder, not wallowing in shame, anger, and guilt, and certainly not doing it like the other kids. In this section we move away from a one-size-fits-all approach and explore six principles to help you create an individualized project-based review. Project-based review is not so much a method or a system, but rather an approach that embraces the different ways we learn and treats each exam as an individual project. By approaching exams systematically, you can make sure you study the most important information in an appropriate way for the type of test you are taking and in a manner that is tailored to your mind. The six principles are: Size and Girth Matter; Application Is the Key to Knowing; Exercise Your Right to Choose; Individualize Your Review; Study Smarter; and Individualize Your Review (Again).

### *Principle 1: Size and Girth Matter*

Knowing the scope and content of your exam is the first step toward a solid review. The scope is plain and simple: it tells you how much you have to know and is pretty easy to find out. To figure out the scope of your exam, go straight to the top, and ask the professor what will be covered on the exam. If that doesn't work, check your review sheet (if available) and your syllabus. Try to be as specific as possible, noting what chapters and readings are covered in the exam. This gives you a tentative idea of how big your exam is going to be.

Still overwhelmed? The next step is to zero in on the specific content that your exam will cover because the content is the core of a solid review. By content, we're talking about the good stuff: the terms, theories, arguments, and concepts that you will be responsible for knowing. No exam will test every concept, every detail, and every theme that the professor explored throughout the semester. In every course, certain information will be identified as priority, and others will be set aside set as secondary (and still more will be abandoned completely). When you know how much is covered and what is covered, you are well on your way to reducing the hours spent in the library. To figure this out, we turn to the power of inference and interpersonal communication. Here is where to look:

- **Ask the prof.** A quick e-mail or a visit during office hours can make or break a review. If you're nervous, suck it up: getting a context for your review is a legitimate academic request. The more you talk about the exam and the content of the course before you drop the big question, the better the odds are that you'll hit gold. Chat it up, and then ask your prof what the content of the exam is going to be. Try to get as specific as possible. Is it going to be terms, themes, concepts, or something else? You may get nowhere, but there is no harm in asking.
- **Go to your review sheet.** If you're lucky, your review sheet may have a section that explicitly outlines the material covered within the exam. This can take on a number of different forms, but, like pornography, you'll know it when you see it. If you are not that lucky, look for anything that appears to be a broad categorical statement concerning the content of the exam—for example, "You will be expected to have reviewed all . . ." You are specifi-

cally looking for words like *themes, terms, concepts, arguments,* and *theories,* in close proximity to words like *expected, evaluate, demonstrate,* and *communicate.*

- **Review your syllabus.** If you do not strike gold with the review sheet, take what you do get and give it some critical thought. Every course has different types of details, theories, and arguments. What type of course are you in, and what is its focus? Try to push past the obvious ("a psych course") toward a more in-depth answer: "a psych course about personality disorders." How has the course progressed (by schools of thought, historical periods, topical areas, or line-by-line according to the textbook)? What are the different headings for each lecture? What type of information has been covered in the lectures, and how have the lectures been structured (details? terms? theories?)? If you were given the broadest of categories, try to fill in an example of each. This is just tentative, so do not stress too much about it.

- **Dig up old exams.** Old exams are perfect for understanding the content of an exam. Hardly any teacher will recycle an exam verbatim, but you can bet they will recycle a common structure. If you get hold of one (the Web is a great place to look; many professors post them), look at how the test is broken down (e.g., term definitions, multiple choice, essay). Also look to see what kind of stuff was tested: terms, concepts, process, and so on. The same type of information will probably come up again, and you now have a good idea of what the content of your exam will be like.

With the content of your exam in mind, even in the rough stages, you have taken a huge step toward reducing the wasted hours in the library and improving your grade.

The next big step is to think about how you are going to use this information. A lot can come from this: more free time, more effective review, and better grades, to name just a few (fame, glory: we could go on and on . . . ).

### Principle 2: Application Is the Key to Knowing

Knowing how we are going to have to perform come exam day (or e-day) is the key to a project-based review. By performance, we mean how we are going to have to apply all the information we are so studiously gathering throughout the course of our review. By looking at the application of information in conjunction with the scope and content of the exam, you can identify what level of critical thought you must give to each piece of information. The level tells you more about what you have to study and what you can let slide. More than just letting you play to the professor's expectations, reviewing in this way lets you engage in real learning. Rather than studying rote information for regurgitation, you are studying for application, which will result in a much higher level of thought.

There are two things that tell us about application. The first is the *type of exam*. Each type of exam demands different levels of critical thought concerning the material that you are reviewing. Asking the prof is again the best way to figure this out. However, if time is of the essence, the structure of your test will be stated in your study guide, your syllabus, or some old test.

Once you have identified the structure of your exam, check out the professor's expectations. All professors have goals or expectations for their course. Words such as *identify, define, compare/contrast, relate, argue, support, refute, apply,* and *think critically* tell you how to use the information that you have so studiously gathered. Not to be redundant, but the best place to get this info is right from the horse's mouth with a simple question: "I was wondering, are we going to have to just define the terms, or are we going to have to compare and contrast

# THE HIGHLY UNORIGINAL CHART

By thinking critically about the type of exam you are about to take, you can learn how you have to use any given piece of information and then what you need to know about that information. The following chart will help you in the process:

| Type of Exam | Application of Information |
| --- | --- |
| Multiple choice | Literal, interpretive |
| Term identification | Literal |
| Problem sets | Application |
| Essay | Application, literal, interpretive |
| Matching | Literal |
| True-false | Interpretive, literal |

TRANSLATING EXPECTATIONS

Three Levels of Comprehension

Literal: facts, statistic, definitions, recognition
Interpretive: causes, effects, and inferences
Application: using information to solve a problem

How well do you need to know what you are studying? The better question is, "What am I going to need to use it for?" Comprehension and assimilation of information isn't black and white; there are a number of ways that we can know what we know.

Source: Kathleen T. McWhorter, Study and Critical Thinking Skills in College (New York: HarperCollins, 1972).

them?" If lack of time or fear rules that out, check out "course goals" and/or "expectations" in your syllabus. While reading it, ask yourself: Does the professor want me to apply it or memorize it? Also, check your syllabus for a statement like this: "The test will force you to apply/define/argue, etc." Last, try the review sheet. The trick is to look for prompts such as, "You will be expected to . . ." or "This exam will require you to . . ."

After giving some thought to how you will have to apply the information on the test, go back and think about the content of your exam. The application changes what and how you have to know the content. Give each piece of information a good review and ask yourself, What do I have to do with this, and what do I have to know about it to be successful come e-day? For example, along with "terms" you should put "define and compare/contrast" if you have to know both their literal definition and their relationship to other terms. That tells you what you have to study and how you have to know this information. Job well done.

Still overwhelmed? One more step before reviewing: checking out choice.

### Principle 3: Exercise Your Right to Choose

Many exams give you a choice of questions to answer. Knowing your choice factor allows you to eliminate things from your review—a good thing, one of the best of things. To figure out your choice factor, check your review sheet specifically in expectations or in the structure of the exam, looking for language like, "You will have the option of answering two out of four essay questions," or "You will have the choice of . . ." You get the point. If your prof has hooked you up with some really good review sheets, once you know the scope and content of the exam, take some steps toward eliminating what your review will cover.

---

## COLLEGE MATH 101

If you figure out that you will be given a choice of essays on the final exam (e.g., you will have to answer two out of five essays), and if your professor's review sheet lists all of the possible questions or specific topical areas ("those five will be selected from the following ten possibilities"), simple math will let you eliminate whole questions safely from the material to be studied. Simply subtract the number of questions that you will ultimately have to answer on the test (two) from the number of options you will have on the test (five). This is the number of questions that you can safely eliminate from the study sheet (a total of three, as long as you know the other questions cold).

Said differently: $n = x - (y - z)$ where $n$ is the number of questions you need to study, $x$ is the total number of potential questions on the professor's review sheet, $y$ is the number of choices you will be given on the exam, and $z$ is the number of questions you will required to answer.

---

### Principle 4: Individualize Your Review

Now it is time to get down to individualizing your review. You stand at a critical juncture: knowing what your exam will cover and how you have to perform come e-day, but with no method for approaching the review process. As we said before, most other study guides tell you to adopt a one-size-fits-all template for reviewing your course material. Their real recommendation is simply to do the reading throughout the semester. We will ignore that fact for now. They recommend study sheets all around the town. But that is not for us.

It is important to have a clear, stable structure to hold the information you worked so hard at digging up. The "I'll remember that" strategy, although somewhat progressive and gaining influence among academics, is not the most effective approach. Trust us; we've tried.

We are not going to tell you what structure to use. There are different types of reviewing methods, each one best for particular types of information and still others better for different types of thinkers. For example, if you've got a bunch of terms on your plate and are facing a multiple choice test, flash cards are the way to go. But if it's an essay exam that is staring you down, the outline format is tool number one. Always keep in mind how you learn and how you are going to have to perform on the exam as you check out the following information review methods. You may need to use only one of these or a few of them, or create you own personalized hybrid:

- **Flash cards.** Using a 3-by-5-inch index card, divide your information into two categories: one side broad, the other specific (or any other dichotomy that seems appropriate). This is a good method for memorizing terms, concepts, people, or any other linear details. This method is good for a test that is going to ask you to identify or define a literal piece of information through recall and recognition—for example, multiple choice, matching, and identification questions. Also, by studying two cards at once, you can prepare for compare-and-contrast questions by asking yourself to identify similarities and differences between the terms.
- **Linear outline.** A numeric and alphabetic outline is used to structure both broad and specific information that is linked together. This type of formal structure is good for identifying concepts, their definitions, and supporting details. This is especially good if you have a tendency to think about information more on the organizational and structural side. It is specifically relevant to essay exams or exams that ask you to understand the specifics of an author's theories or arguments.

- **Box outline.** Very similar to the linear outline, but more spatial and less hierarchical, it allows for more visual memory integration while retaining the structural clarity of the linear outline. It is good for review of specific but complicated topics for application on essay exams.
- **Concept map.** One step beyond the box outline, it abandons linear relationships completely and allows ideas to exist spatially while maintaining the integrity of their interconnections. This is a method for understanding the class holistically and is most relevant to final essay exams that ask you to synthesize the material presented over the course and for any essay that asks you to convey large and interconnected ideas. It also can be an initial brainstorming and organizing tool for those who think spatially and laterally, as well as a tool to be referred to in later steps.
- **Recursive step outline.** This is best for math and science exams that require you to know the logical steps in a complex process and is most applicable to tests that require you to solve problems. This structure helps you map the steps for any process (step 1, how it leads to step 2, etc.).
- **Thematic review sheet.** This relies on the structure of two-column notes. The goal is to approach the course thematically—to identify the dominant themes of the course and then to support each with a detail, example, or explanation. This is useful for an overall review of the course, and specifically for exams that will test you on your ability to understand themes.

With this structure or structures in hand, it is time to gather the answers. We are going to let you in on a little secret right now: organizing information in a manner congruent with how you will have to use it and how your mind learns is a huge step toward learning it cold. You are on the home stretch.

### Principle 5: Study Smarter

We have spent so much time setting up our review that there is no way we are now going to waste our time doing useless reading or studying. Every course stresses some ideas or information over others, as does every textbook, and the key to studying smarter is to get the most important information first and the least important last. Pretty simple. Venture into the least important zone only if you have time on your hands or are so Ritted up that your eyes are about to pop out and you can't sleep.

If you follow this through to the end, you should give yourself a big pat on your whatever, because you are now surfing toward the top of the grade curve. Remind yourself of how much information you have to know, what type of information is on the exam, and what you have to know about this information. Here is how we go looking for answers:

- **Identify primary sources.** Every test comes from somewhere; the trick is to figure out what somewhere this test comes from the most. Many professors lecture all year, only to test you right out of the book. Others give reading after reading, only to test you on the lecture. Still others focus in on one textbook and ignore the others. To identify the primary source of your exam, review some old exams or critically read the syllabus, paying close attention to any source that takes up a large amount of time. For the best results, however, go to the prof and ask, "So, will the exam come mostly from lecture or from our readings. If from the readings, which ones?" If you do not ask, you cannot receive. It is totally cool to do this.
- **Take a body count.** Before jumping into any review, scan your syllabus, identifying any readings, lectures, and concepts that you understand completely and any that you do not understand at all.

- **Skim textbooks.** Textbook writers love to give you the answers and do so in every chapter summary. Chapter summaries give you all the terms, main ideas, and primary theories covered in the chapter. Depending on the scope of the exam, reread the relevant chapter summaries, focusing on the information that is relevant to your test. Record anything that stands out visually (e.g., boldface or italic type). Also, skim the chapter for each item that you recorded, read the paragraph your item is in, the paragraph before it, and the paragraph after it. Again record any relevant information.

- **Skim notes.** Review your notes by cross-checking the information from your summary review and looking for red flags—information that your professor identified during lecture as likely material for exam questions. Ideally, you may have already identified red flags while taking notes (see Chapter 4, "Taking Notes Further"). If not, go through your notes and look for concepts that are repeated or otherwise emphasized. To cross check, go to your note summaries if you have them (see Chapter 4), or skim your notes looking for the information that you extracted from your summary review. A good way to skim your notes is to focus on broad categories, letting details slide. Mark as important anything that appears in both your notes and the chapter summary (that means both the professor and the book thought it was important—two times is the charm), and add any new information from your notes to what you got out of the summary.

- **Go to the syllabus.** Critically read the syllabus for any subheading or class title that looks unfamiliar to you. For ones that you do not recognize right off the bat, review your notes, and skim the readings assigned for that class. Again, record any relevant information according to your master review sheet.

- **Think about homework.** Workbook assignments, problem sets, and any other prior assignments (within the scope of the test) are all prime sources of good information. Critically read each question, and ask yourself what it is getting at, or, if it is a math or science question, what the process is behind it. This will most likely be a broad statement such as, "The question tested my knowledge of behavior theorists." Also, using the answers to the questions from the answer key or from corrections, do a problem-based skim by reading the table of contents and then all section heads. When you find the section that contains either the broad category or the specific answer, read the paragraph it is in, the one before it, and the one after it.

- **Go to the head of the class.** The goal is to run by the professor what you have already ascertained in an effort to see if you have left anything out, and if so, where you can get that information. The best way to do this is to come clean with how much you have studied—specifically, how *hard* you have studied—and ask her where the holes in your knowledge are. Active questions (see Chapter 5, "Dominate Discussion") work great here.

- **Use your peers.** Run by your peers where you stand, and see if they can give you an idea about any of the holes that need to be filled with large ideas.

---

## ORGANIZING THE STUDY GROUP THAT DOESN'T SUCK

Study groups are infamous on university campus. How many times have you wandered to a dorm room in search of exam answers, only to realize that no one knows what the hell is going on? These groups have high potential, but most of the time they simply peter out. However, if you take the right approach you can realize the full potential of the study group. Here are some guiding principles for organizing the study group that doesn't suck:

## PRINCIPLE 1: DEFINE YOUR GOALS

This is the biggest of them all. Too often we jump into the study group with little idea of what we are looking to get out of it. Take a second to define your goals clearly for the group, to the point of outlining specific information and content that you hope to ascertain. Time spent here is time well spent.

## PRINCIPLE 2: DO SOME REVIEW

No, we are not talking actually doing the reading, although it couldn't hurt. All we're talking about here is taking a second to get a context for the class. We all remember information better when we know how it all fits together.

## PRINCIPLE 3: KNOW YOUR LEARNING STYLES

If you learns by reading information, the study group, no matter how well organized, will suck. If talking helps you learn, jump on in, head first. The moral of the story is to give some thought to how you learn best in order to make a decision about the effectiveness of a study group for you.

## PRINCIPLE 4: SET A TIME LIMIT

No study group was meant to last forever. Set a time limit, follow that time limit, and then move on.

With this done, all that is left to do is to get this stuff into your long-term memory.

### Principle 6: Individualize Your Review (Again)

This last principle brings us down the home stretch. Studying for your exam may seem like a daunting task, so it is pep talk time. You are already well on your way to remembering the information for the exam. Throughout this process, you actively engaged with the material from the course by identifying priority information and organizing it in a way that is congruent with how you are going to have to know it. Your mind is now well prepared to move on to reviewing and retaining the material for the exam.

The goal of this principle is to get the information into your head by individualizing your review approach. Following are some ways to engage your study method more effectively to ensure that you learn the material cold:

- **Fondle your flash cards.** If you have a set of flash cards with terms, theories, or whatever, you are probably looking to get this information into your head to the level of recall. The trick is how you go about learning these cards. To ensure effective memorization, make two piles as you review: an "I-know-it-inside-and-out" pile and an "I-don't-know-shit" pile. As you review, sort the cards into the appropriate pile. Every other time through the cards, go back over the "know it" pile and review. Also, if you started with terms and went to definitions, make sure you switch and go the other way too. Make sure you shuffle the cards. Our minds are damn good at memorizing associations and patterns, so we need to be sure to jolt them once in a while. Also, use color to identify cards that always mess you up, and try incorporating a visual to help you remember. Do them out loud and walk around.

- **Nuzzle your notes.** When going over review sheets, have something that allows you to divide specific information from categorical information. As you move down the review sheet, cover up information and quiz yourself on the answers. Again, use color as you see fit. Also, on a separate piece of paper, record any questions you had concerning the information. Attempt to answer the question. Again, make sure the oral mode is in effect here.
- **Pet your problem sets.** Answer the questions; then turn the answers into their own questions (so you will know the information backwards and forwards). Cover up, highlight difficult and important aspects of each step, and do problem sets.
- **Ogle your outlines.** If you have outlined an essay or concept, attempt to recite it to yourself. Also, practice doing the outline from memory, identifying any difficult spots with color.

Not only can you engage with the structure of our review more effectively, but you can also get more of your mind involved, always a good thing for the GPA. Check out these multiple entry points to help remember information and see how you can achieve multiple academic stimulation:

- **Color it.** Color is a great way to identify priority information and help the information stay in your head. This might mean using colored flash cards, colored pencils, or a rainbow of highlighters. Before you review, try identifying specific colors for themes, details, concepts, and arguments. Color also lets you highlight pieces of information that continue to give you trouble or that you have a tendency to overlook.
- **Draw it.** Try supplementing written material with visual representation. Specifically, this may be useful in science classes for descriptions of specific processes or in history classes for

diagramming maps and political developments. Try using shapes or rubber stamps to make nonlinear concept maps.

- **Talk about it.** Recite information out loud when reviewing almost anything. Try tape-recording yourself and playing the tape back.
- **Touch it.** Try to find ways to engage with the material physically to access your tactile and kinesthetic memory. Work at a big table so you can move things around, group flash cards, or build models. Alternately, try integrating physical movement into the act of studying. Trace concepts with your hand, draw concept maps on a whiteboard, walk around when reciting information, and chew gum or drink massive amounts of liquids any time you are reading or sitting. All of these engage your physical memory system.

---

### OUR FAVORITE STUDY TIP

According to Jacobs and McNeely (1992), information learned at the point of orgasm during sexual intercourse has a 98 percent likelihood of being retained for later use. We don't make this stuff up. We just report it.

---

- **Personalize it.** When reviewing, relate new information to your life. Try to compare it to things that you have learned in the past, or relate it to your life experience. For example, try relating every term to a personal anecdote.
- **Use it.** Force yourself to apply the information by using it to solve a problem or answer a question. This is *especially* relevant for science and math class. See Problem Solution Exams, page 218.

With your review method individualized, all that is left is putting in the hours. Time to get caffeinated and Ritted up, and get ready to destroy your exam.

## THE FOOD AND DRUG ADMINISTRATION

While we come down fully in favor of caffeine binges and sugar loading, watch yourself. Stress, combined with a lack of sleep and poor all-around nutrition (i.e., finals) plus a sleep/coffee/ Ritt crash, is really hard on the body and the mind. In order to avoid hospitalization (at least until after exams) throw these ideas into the mix:

- **Delay the madness.** The further into studying for exams that you can start the caffeine and all-nighters, the better off you are. They will be more effective, and you will be less likely to burn out completely.
- **Drink like a fish.** Water, that is. Staying hydrated is the most important nutritional step to take during finals. Buy a big bottle of water, and keep it next to you when you study. Nervous habit will take care of the rest. (Water is even more important if your pre-exam reading period included a party; alcohol consumption leaves you dehydrated for days afterward.)
- **Eat.** High-protein and complex carbohydrates are key here—PB&J works, as do Power Bars, Balance Bars, Slim-Fast shakes, and cold cereal. (Also remember to pick up the 7-Eleven major food groups: orange juice, bananas, salted nuts, water, yogurt, and cheese.)
- **Move.** Time taken to get a little exercise during exam time is time well spent. Concentration improves, as do retention and alertness.

. . .

This concludes the six principles for a project-based review. If you follow this approach for any exam, you will learn your material better and in less time than spending days pulling levers. However, although this is a comprehensive approach, there still are specialized types of exams that we need to turn our attention to. In Section 2, we outline insider tips for every other type of exam out there.

### Section 2: Studying Under Special Circumstances

Unfortunately, we do not have any exciting special circumstances to explore, although we tried our damnedest to outline "How to Study on an Acid Trip." We also do not have any more approaches up our sleeves, but we do have some tips to improve your review for extenuating circumstances.

In this section we give you the inside dirt on cramming like a pro, reviewing for take-home and open-note exams, reviewing for essay exams, and reviewing for problem solution exams (for all you scientists out there). With your principles in hand, here we go, and remember: keep what works, shun the rest, but tell your friends to buy the book.

#### Cramming Like a Pro

We just walked through a time-intensive approach for reviewing for exams. For now, throw it out the window, because it is reality-check time. We all cram for exams, more times than we like, but it happens. Is it a bad thing? This question is irrelevant. It happens, and the most important thing is not dwelling on the pros and cons of cramming, but rather getting it done in the most effective way possible. For us, a "cram" is reviewing for a difficult exam (one where you know less than half of the info required) in twenty-four hours or less. When the clock starts ticking and your blood pressure skyrockets, here is how to cram like a pro:

- **Understand the limitations, and let them go.** Cramming is not the best way to study for an exam, but why dwell on this in the moment? Shame is a great motivator, but we will leave that for all the elementary school teachers in the world. When you begin a cram, try to put the self-loathing aside, acknowledge you are starting at a deficit, let it go, and move on. Concentrate on the present, doing the best you can, getting through the night. That is all that matters for now.
- **Manage your time.** When the clock is ticking, time management is of the utmost importance. A good rule of thumb is to wipe your day clean of all obligations. Spend a little under half of your allotted review time on organizing the information and the rest on getting it into memory. For more tips on time management, see the Planning the Productive All-Nighter box.

---

## PLANNING THE PRODUCTIVE ALL-NIGHTER

We all do it, all the time, every semester, every year, sometimes just to say we did: the collegiate all-nighter. However, regardless of the all-nighter's bragging potential, it does have a legitimate purpose. Sometimes, for whatever reason, staying up all night is a damn good idea. On these days and nights, follow the following to use those precious twenty-four hours the best you can:

- **Power nap schedule.** This can be used as an alternative to an all-nighter or in tandem, but Jon discovered in the writing of this book that you can function at a high cognitive level for over a month by getting three hours of sleep a

night and then taking four twenty-minute naps throughout the day (he stole this idea from President Clinton). If
you must venture into the night, try that trick, or simply
the idea of taking power naps throughout the process.

- **Dumb down.** The key to an effective all-nighter is how you
  space out the type of material you engage with and the
  tasks you do. A good rule of thumb is that by 5 A.M. it is
  best to be studying the simplest material and doing the
  simplest task out there. This is not the time to learn quan-
  tum physics.

- **Set goals.** Pretty simple: before you head into the night,
  know why you are doing so and what you hope to get out of
  it. A concrete task list gives you something to turn to in the
  wee hours.

- **Get set up.** Another simple but overlooked step. An all-
  nighter is only as good as its set-up. Choose a place away
  from your bed. Bring with you food, medication, caffeine,
  and you're ready to ride black beauty into the night.

- **Eat.** No matter how nauseous you feel as the night wanes
  and the day breaks, eat some food. Your sanity will thank
  you.

- **Get out.** We discovered the power of this one writing in the
  dead of winter in Providence, but a brisk midnight walk or
  just a run up a set of stairs is a perfect energy booster.

- **Conceptualize.** The first step in cramming is to get a
  broad framework for your exam in your mind. As you
  rush for information, a broad framework acts as a holding
  pen by giving your mind some way to organize the material. First, read your syllabus, paying close attention to the
  course description and all headings. What is this course
  about? Take a moment to run it through your mind: the
  lectures, the reading, the professor. Don't worry if you do
  not remember everything. Then take a moment to note

the content of your exam, its scope, and the type of test you are taking (see Principles 1, 2, and 3). With the class fresh in your mind, ask yourself, If you were giving the test, what would you cover? (If you found some old exams, look at these and see what questions were asked.)

- **Eliminate information.** The trick now is getting the main ideas—nothing more. This is tricky because each class has a different focus. With no mercy, skim your textbooks and notes, and squeeze your peers for the most important concepts, events, and so on. Some rules of thumb for this: if you know the breakdown of the test (what sections are worth the most), make sure you cover those with an appropriate amount of effort. Also, consult your syllabus and focus on text or concepts that get the most class attention. In the end, though, you have to go with your gut.

- **Less is more.** With the priority information in hand, the next challenge is to memorize as much of it as possible. However, it is more important to know one-third of the information cold than to have a rough understanding of all of it. Try to identify a manageable chunk of information to memorize/know. Stay with this until you have it down cold, and only then move on. Trust us. This calculated risk pays off come exam time.

With these tips in mind, cram away. Remember, a test is a test is a test, and there is always another one around the corner. (We have no idea what that means.)

### Reviewing for Take-Home and Open-Note Exams

Take-home and open-note exams are a good, good thing. Both require you to apply or synthesize information as opposed to simply regurgitating it. If you get one of these, here is how to take advantage of the opportunity.

- **Do a review.** Although these tests do allow you access to class notes and readings, you get more out of the test and do better if you take the time to review or cram before the day of the exam.
- **Think big picture.** The vast majority of take-home and open-note exams are concerned with applying or analyzing complex themes and concepts. While you review, focus on the big picture. A good way to do this is to create a concept map that outlines all the major ideas for the class. Use whatever best floats your alternative learning style boat. We use a mind map form.
- **Memorize themes, concepts, and other big stuff.** In review, spend your time on the big ideas of the class. These are what you will be tested on, and come exam day it's hard to learn them by skimming through a book.
- **Flag detail; don't memorize.** In your review, do not waste time memorizing details, terms, or other minutiae. However, do spend time flagging these details in your reading and notes. A sticky note works great; on it, write the name of the detail and where it fits in the big picture.
- **Create a master review sheet.** For both of these types of exam, having information in a central and accessible space is a life and grade saver. Instead of spending hours memorizing information, write it all down on one or two pages. Make sure you include page numbers from your readings and lecture notes. Use whatever note form works for your mind.

For take-home exams only, also consider:

- **Annotate essays.** For take-home exams, do not outline essays completely in the review period. If you have a review sheet that includes possible essay questions, use it as a review tool, and do a key word outline: thesis and main points for paragraphs. That is all.

- **Skim readings.** With take-homes you have some more liberty on what texts get thoroughly skimmed for review and what texts you only glance over. Any texts that you deem secondary should get only a glance. If come e-day, you were wrong about the importance of a reading, you can skim the reading in a pinch.
- **Know parameters.** With take-homes, it is important to understand the parameters of the exam: the format, how long the answers should be, and whether outside research will be required.

### Essay Exams

The dreaded essay exam is a source of much stress and anxiety in the Mooney and Cole reality. When review comes along, we know there is a lot out there that needs to be covered, but we are not quite sure what it is or how to get it all down. Not as easy as copying down a bunch of terms, the essay exam requires complex thinking skills. But that is the good part. We've got the tough angle covered (the complex thinking skills), and all we need is the structure and approach. Here are some things to consider when preparing for essay exams:

- **Review from broad to specific.** An essay exam is all about connections, ideas, concepts, and relationships. In reviewing, focus primarily on the course as a whole and the big stuff running throughout it. If possible, try to give the course a thesis. What concept did it try to argue? And how did it do so? The syllabus is as good a place as any to start.
- **Practice looking for a thesis.** The key to an essay is a thesis, so as you review, look at your notes for the day, or go over the readings, constantly trying to identify the thesis driving the information. Try to give each lecture and

reading a thesis. If you have time, run these by your prof, and see what she or he thinks.

- **Anticipate questions.** If you were not given a list of possible essay questions, try to turn every reading or class into a question. Ask yourself, "What could the prof possibly ask me from this reading/lecture/information?" The broader, the better.
- **Outline.** If you have your essay topics in advance and you have some time on your hands, do a key word outline. Each paragraph gets five sentences: the paragraph's main point, three supporting details, and then a transition statement. You visual thinkers can try mapping your outline. Also give a color to main points and evidence to help recall.
- **Do dry runs.** For review, don't just read your outlines; do them from memory. Do them out loud and while walking around. The more movement, the better.

Keep this stuff in mind for any essay exam, and fear not the written word.

### *Problem Solution Exams*

This is our last stop on the reviewing train. This, much like the reading method, is for all of you who love differential equations (who doesn't?). When trig, advanced algebra, and organic chemistry fill your finals schedule, here are some things to consider:

- **Don't read; do.** Reading your chapters, problem sets, and problem solutions is useless and a waste of time. Start with the problems. Work backward to solve them, reading the text when required. Check your work when you are done.

- **Identify types of problems.** As you work, organize a review sheet around types of problems you encounter. For each problem, give an example and an outline of the process or steps necessary to solve the problem. A flash card is good for this.
- **Go over homework.** Old problem sets are golden for this review. Go over these closely, looking for your mistakes. Once you find one, solve it, going back into the text if necessary. Pay close attention to what you screwed up on in terms of its highest value.
- **Centralize.** With the glory of Stalin or Chairman Mao in one centralized space, write out all formulas, equations, and other stuff necessary for the exam. Color is good, specifically red.
- **Build it.** If you are the touchy-feely type and learn by building, try getting a chemistry set to build your problems. After you break the problem down, each piece gets a block, and you put it all together as you solve it. A great way to get the tactical memory going.

That concludes problem-based review and also concludes the section on reviewing for specialized exams. The home stretch awaits. On to summary time, which, as we all know, is good time. You stop reading. We stop writing. What could possibly be better than that?

SUMMARY

The core of this chapter was project-based review—six principles to help you create an individualized review that honors the demands of your exam and the individual style of your mind. After that, we explored good down-home tips for specialized reviews and our favorite, the cram (cram and be proud). But most important, the tip to tell the folks about, we learned that orgasm is a powerful study tool, permanently embedding information on your cerebral cortex. So with tests in hand, go forth and review. Bye-bye. All done. Adios. Good night, sweet prince.

# 9: Beating the Exam Game

No matter how hard you've reviewed, whether you've followed the principles for individualized project-based review, flashed your flash cards, outlined, read, reread, done interpretive dance, prayed, used our favorite study tip, or sacrificed small animals, there is no way to get around the fact that exams are a major pain in the ass. If you do enjoy taking exams, you're reading the wrong book and should check out our forthcoming work on masochism. Our frustration with exams stems from the fact that they are a stupid way to evaluate students' learning. All exams by their nature (with the exception of open-ended essay exams) are standardized—a one-size-fits-all attempt to impose empirical standards on learning and dedication, which cannot be measured empirically. These standardized temples unfortunately hold the key to so much: our GPA and often our self-esteem.

As we all know, "objectivity" is an artificial construct, and there are many variables that go into our success or failure at exams that many professors just do not acknowledge. Many students do recall information best through verbal questions, not written prompts. Others cannot write out their answers well, but are best at talking them through. Others students may know information cold, but come test time, test anxiety strikes. Some teachers, like Paulk, our favorite Ivy League professor, believe that all test anxiety is simply a failure by the student to get information to the level of recall. We have some sympathy for him, for it is too bad that his mind does not overflow with connections, emotions, images, times, places, and ideas with a simple prompt from a short answer.

Many times in our lives, overwhelmed with ideas and haunted by the ghosts of two kids who were abused by exams our whole lives, we walked out of tests we spent days preparing for. Dave did not finish one in-class essay throughout all fifteen years of school.

We don't walk out of exams any more, although nothing has changed within the academy's approach to testing. In college, the multiple choice test has hit our desk many times. What has changed is our approach to taking exams. Exams are not a reflection of our intelligence and are not an accurate reflection of what we know. We approach an exam as a game that has rules and tricks to help us master it. Thus, this chapter is pure cold-hearted pragmatism. In Section 1, we look at the most effective way to do last-minute preparation. In Section 2, we show you how to add points to your score before you answer a single question. In Section 3 we give you good habits for any exam and then explore principles for approaching specific types of exams. In Section 4, we see how we can learn from our test results.

## SECTION 1: LAST-MINUTE PREPARATION

Regardless of what stage of reviewing you are in—even if you are frantically cramming and haven't covered everything—when you get to within an hour and a half of the exam, it's time to stop. The odds of your going over anything at that moment that you will actually retain are slim to none. The hour and an half before an exam can be spent much more effectively than by obsessing over the material. The key is to use this time to prepare emotionally, physically, and practically.

### Emotional Preparation

When you hit the hour and a half mark, put everything down. We know you will be itching for that last review, but we'll get to that. The goal here is to try and gain a little bit of perspective and allow your gourds to process all the information you stuffed into it over the last couple of days. Anxiety can be a great motivating and focusing force, or it can paralyze you. Figure out what level your anxiety is at. If your anxiety has really gotten you onto your game and you are in hyperfocus mode, skip down to getting practically and physically prepared. If, on the other hand, you are feeling overwhelmed, anxious, and obsessive, give the following a try:

- **Get out.** Get out of your study space. If it's your house, get out of your house; if it's the library, get out of the library. Find a relaxing environment and sit down for a few minutes—outdoors, your room, whatever works for you. *Warning:* If you have been up cramming for two days, avoid beds. Take it from guys who know firsthand that almost nothing is as painful as sleeping through an exam, especially one you were well prepared for.
- **Relax and review.** Once out of your study space, try to think of something that relaxes you. It might be a place, a memory, a friend, an experience (remembering our initiation into the mile-high club works well). Wherever you are, try to let this image run through your head. Take some deep breaths, kick back, maybe stretch a little. The goal is to get as relaxed as possible. After a few minutes of running this image through your head, think back over your review. Try to remember the flash cards you used, the books, the underlining, the essays. If you mapped out the review, try to remember the map, the colors, and so on. This is not an exam. Just let the stuff come up.
- **End it.** Try to imagine closing the study session. You're done studying, and that's a good thing. You are prepared. Think about going into the exam feeling confident and happy. You will soon be finished with the exam and will have done a really good job.

- **Think positively.** Try to imagine yourself nailing the exam. Imagine getting questions you know the answers to, expressing yourself clearly and concisely, and feeling good about your performance. And think about being done with the exam. Envision how it'll feel to be done, what you'll do after, and where you'll go to celebrate later.

We hope these exercises will have cut your blood pressure in half, so now it's time to get ready to get examined.

### *Get Armed: Material Preparation*

Get all your stuff together. If you have a hard time remembering things or it takes you a long time to get out the door, leave an hour for this. Make a list the night before the exam, and put it right by your book bag or whatever else always goes with you to class. Here are some things that you may want to or should bring:

- A writing utensil of some kind
- A second writing utensil for when the first one breaks, runs out of ink, or gets lost on a mini-break
- Some paper
- Books and notes (if it's an open-book or open-notes test)
- Computer, if your accommodations allow it
- Highlighter
- An index card or ruler to cover up questions other than the one you are answering (we'll get back to this one)
- Food: Gummi Bears, dried fruit, a Power Bar—available, effective, and easy to eat on the sly if your proctor is a real stiff
- A fidget widget (something to play with)

With this stuff in hand, you're set to get pumped for the exam.

## *Getting Jacked: Physical Preparation*

Physical preparation is often the step that gets left out. More often than not, we stumble out of bed or peel ourselves off our desk chair to arrive at the exam underslept, hungry, and suffering from a wicked caffeine hangover. Although common, this is not the optimal test-taking state. By taking the following simple steps, you can ensure that you are ready to go like your frontal lobe is on Viagra when the exam hits your desk. Here's what we do, usually about an hour before the exam:

- **The five-minute power nap.** This is a risky one (as we said, sleeping through an exam sucks), so you'll have to give some critical thought to whether this is a good idea. The idea is to set an alarm for a little over five minutes right by your head. Then put your head down. You will not actually fall asleep, but you will get up feeling refreshed. If you are a heavy sleeper, ax this tip.
- **Eat.** About a half-hour before the exam, have something light (e.g., yogurt and a bagel or cereal and fruit; get some protein in there somewhere). This will get your blood sugar charged up and leave you with plenty of time to work through the food hangover—the lapse of energy right after eating, when the blood goes to your stomach.
- **Caffeinate.** Down the hatch, but only a cup or two. You don't want to get the shakes.
- **Ritt it up.** If you take medication, do it about a half-hour before the exam to give your frontal lobe a wake-up call that will have time to hit by the exam.
- **Do a little aerobic activity.** You could do a set or two of push-ups or a few sit-ups, or go for a brisk walk right before the exam. (If your exam is in a tall building, run up and down the stairs.) Getting your heart rate up gets

blood to the cabeza and helps to relieve stress and reduce anxiety—all good things.

- **Warm up mentally.** With about half an hour left to go or on your way to the exam, take about ten minutes to read through all of your material again out loud. We stress *read;* don't quiz, obsess, or try to rehearse through interpretive dance. Just read it. You're only warming up your brain. Alternatively, set your material aside and read something short and provocative that has nothing to do with the exam. A newspaper or magazine article can give a needed reminder that this test is not all that exists in the world and get the neurons firing at the same time. With that done, take a deep breath and go off to class.

SECTION 2: ADD POINTS BEFORE YOU BEGIN

Time spent preparing yourself before you begin your test can add points to your final score. The key is to engage with the test and the testing environment from the moment you walk into the classroom. This means getting situated, getting the lay of the land by scanning the test, and then prereading and planning.

### Getting Situated

Time spent right before the exam can make or break the test. Arrive early and do the following:

- **Make sure you're accommodated.** For all of you out there with accommodations, arriving early gives you the time to make sure you are getting what you expect and deserve. Approach the professor before the room is crowded, and subtly remind him or her of the accommodations that you are going to receive. Say something to the effect of, "I really appreciate your understanding and willingness to work with me in terms of my academic accommodations by [insert accommodations]." Nine out of ten times, this will make your prof feel good about hooking you up. And if he or she forgot, this is a chance to "suddenly remember" and still look accommodating and helpful. If you don't get what you expected, be prepared how to respond. See the Aborting Illegal Exams box.

---

## ABORTING ILLEGAL EXAMS

If you get a blank stare or a response from your prof that indicates that you are not receiving the accommodations you were expecting for the exam, you need to up the ante a little. First, make sure you are correct about what you were promised. If so, say something to the effect of, "I do appreciate [insert the partial accommodation that they are giving], but it was my understanding that I would also receive [the accommodation you expected]." If you still don't get a favorable response, ask to speak with the prof in private (this will let him or her know you are serious, and not simply asking for this stuff because it is easy to get). Decide whether you are going to take the exam without the full accommodations or leave. It is within your rights under the law to walk out of the classroom and refuse to take a test under inaccessible conditions. But you may be in for a fight.

---

- **Get priority seating.** Get the priority seat. If you are in the exam room, try to get one away from windows and doors, which are potential distractions. Also, if you need to take breaks, sit on an aisle.

- **Warm up.** As you are waiting for the exam, try to do a lit-tle writing or brainstorming on a piece of paper. This is specifically helpful if you historically have struggled with getting started or with writing essays. If you are writing, jot down a sentence about something that you were en-gaged by in your material. Next, try writing out what your goals for the test are (grade, etc.). You can also just try to describe the atmosphere—what the prof is wearing, or which of your peers look as if they were visited by the angel of death, for example. If you're brainstorming, just let the associations go.

If you still have time on your hands, just chill out and wait. The test will hit your desk soon enough.

### Test in Hand: Prereading and Planning

Caught with your test in your hand right now is not a bad thing. However, don't get too excited and jump into the act just yet. Time spent before you answer any question will improve your grade. Guaranteed. When your test hits your desk, con-sider doing the following:

- **Listen.** When the prof starts giving instructions, stop whatever you are doing. Have a separate piece of paper handy to record questions. Whenever the prof references the test, look where directed and record down anything that is said. In this case, listen very carefully for the words *mistake, forgot, correction,* or *choice.* These cues will al-most always draw your attention to something very perti-nent to the exam. Don't be afraid to write down any words that he or she uses that don't make sense to you. Also, if you do have a question, phrase it actively. This is a good time to remember the active questions drill from Chapter 5, "Dominate Discussion." Identify what puzzles you, break it down in terms of what you understand and do not understand, and then phrase your question actively using this simple structure: "I understand $x$, but I don't understand $y$."

- **Get on the same page.** Some things to think about or clarify before you begin are: Who will keep track of time? Will they give you reminders starting from the last half-hour? Can you take breaks, and do they need to be supervised? And if you are using accommodations like a computer, can you use a dictionary for essay exams? Is an electronic one allowed? What do you do with the test when it is done? Should it be on computer, disk, or hard copy? If on hard copy, where will you print?

- **Scan the test.** Your first task is to preread the test (unless you already know the structure of the exam and looking ahead just makes you nervous—in which case skip to the next point). When you preread, you are looking for the specific sections of the exam. Often these are identified with numbers or letters or in boldface type. For each section, see how much it is worth, how many questions there are, and, if possible, a recommendation on time (e.g., "Section I should take twenty minutes of your time").

- **Make a plan of attack.** Now that you know the structure of the exam, plan your approach. Most people would say that you should start with the easiest questions to get your mind going and begin with a feeling of success. For a lot of us, this is a great idea. We can have a hard time getting started, and our brains take a little while to get into the swing of things. For others the difficulty is the opposite: we tire out by the end of the test and have lost the ability to do any hard-core thinking; about all we can do is the easy stuff. If your attention is shot after focusing for too long, start with the more complicated intellectual questions like essays or multistep problems; then return to the easier questions when you are running low on energy. If your exam mostly consists of essays, outline them all first, so you don't have to do any major thinking when you have to write the last one and can barely move.

- **Planning time.** The principle here is pragmatic, pragmatic, pragmatic. What is worth the most points will probably take the longest amount of time. If you have the scoring breakdown, a good rule of thumb is that the percentage of your grade that each section is worth is equal to the amount of time you should spend on that section. For example, in an hour exam, an essay worth 50 percent of the grade should take thirty minutes. If you had double time, it should take an hour. After reviewing your test, plan accordingly.

- **Clear your mind.** Before you answer a single question, dump any information from your review that you feel you may forget on the top of your exam—like formulas, dates, equations, theories, and so forth. Not only does this ensure you'll have it when needed, but it gets the mind going and ready to test.

Time is passing by now. There is nothing left to do but take the test. Following are some fundamental principles and a series of specific strategies for the different types of exams you will encounter.

## SECTION 3: TEST TAKING

Although at first glance, it may seem as though every test is different, in reality, many exams are fundamentally structured in the same way. How many different exams have you taken where you had multiple choice questions, true-false questions, and an essay question? Knowing this, we can apply some fundamental principles to any test we take. The more specific the exam, the more specific the tips. In this section we look at fundamental principles for any exam and then specific strategies for particular types of exams.

### Tips for Any Exam

Following are some tips for every exam you take:

*Tip 1: Critically Read Directions.* Anytime you are given a direction on an exam, bust out your pen and highlighter and engage with them. First, read the directions out loud and follow them with your fingers. Read them twice. The second time through, highlight or underline anything that you do not understand—a word, a sentence, or a whole paragraph. If you have a question, make sure you take a second to phrase it in a way that will get you results, and raise your hand: no fear at all. Answering questions is what the proctor gets paid for. Also, during your second read, focus on language that is demanding something from you. Pay close attention to any list or specific statement. Before moving on, say in your own words what you think the instructions are demanding of you. If you want, call the lackey TA over to listen to you and confirm that you are understanding the directions correctly.

*Tip 2: The Cover-up.* As you move through the exam, cover up everything above or below the question that you are answering. Covering up other questions helps if the page has a tendency to do a little dance in that genius mind of yours, or if you get distracted or overwhelmed by more than one question at a time. You can do this with a blank piece of paper or an index card. If you really want to hot-rod your card, cut out a line in it big enough for one line of text, and take it one line at a time. Using a colored card also helps to highlight the question you are trying to focus on.

*Tip 3: Touch Base Every Five Questions.* If you are using any sort of answer key that is separate from the questions, especially if you are taking a ScanTron test, stop and make sure you are on target every five questions. We have heard horror stories about kids who missed seeing one question and bombed the entire test by putting the rest of the answers in the wrong places.

*Tip(s) 4: Answer What You Know; Play the Guessing Game; Leave Nothing Blank.* As you move through the test, answer what you know first. Anything that is at all unclear or that you just do not know, leave blank and mark the question with something obvious, like a highlighter. After you are done with the test or the section, go back through the unanswered questions. If you know them, you're set. Do not change an answer unless you have a good reason to, such as remembering new information. Your first instinct is right 90 percent of the time. If not, try to think about the following before guessing or leaving it blank: Will you be penalized for wrong answers? Can you eliminate any options (see specific tests for cues)?

If you will not be penalized for incorrect answers, try to eliminate and then guess regardless of what you know. If you will be penalized and can eliminate half the options, guess. If not, move on and chalk one up in the loss category. In classes that do not penalize you for wrong answers, guess at everything, and we mean *everything*. Even if you go completely blank, write down a series of ideas for an essay, or some very simple terms for a short answer. Try whatever is necessary to get something down on the page.

*Tip 5: Review.* There is always time for review. Even if you are the last person in the class and the teacher is about to strangle you, take thirty seconds and do the following:

- Make sure your name is on the exam.
- Make sure you answered all the questions.

- If something is unanswered and you will not be penalized for wrong answers, guess.

If you have some more time, do the following:

- Make sure your answers are legible.
- Make sure all the answers are in the right place on the answer key.
- Review each answer. Change it only if you see that you have made a blatant error.
- Read over your essays.

If your handwriting is like Einstein's (horrible), ask the proctor to spot-check your exam before you leave the room to see if your answers are legible. If they are not, take a second to rewrite whatever is necessary.

These tips are proven to get you better grades. Have faith in them, and they will guide you like the Force. Now, just when you thought we were all out of the good stuff, here comes more. The more specific the exam, the more specific the tips (you've got to love late industrial capitalism and specialization). What follows are specific tips for essay exams, multiple choice, short answer, matching, and true-false.

### Essay Exams

The essay questions are the big one. They are a pain in the ass, but are required for most advanced classes and are traditionally worth the most points in an exam. Moreover, essay exams require advanced levels of critical thought in a short amount of time. However, essays, like any other formulaic test, have a structure, and where there is a structure, there are hints to maximize your effectiveness.

- **Know the question.** Essays are primarily graded on how thoroughly you answer the question. As with all other exams, roll up your sleeves, and grab the directions by the throat. You're specifically looking to isolate the topic, key words about the topic, and focusing words. Also, watch out for essay questions that have many parts. Try to isolate the parts with color. As you search, underline what you don't understand, and ask for clarification. In your own words and out loud, articulate what the exam is asking you to write about.

- **Develop a thesis-driven response.** The thesis is the key to a good essay, so time spent gathering and then forming your ideas into a coherent thesis is very important. If you have some time on your hands during the exam, go through a brainstorming process. Keep this quick, though: your goal is to have a thesis statement done within the first ten minutes of starting the essay. Keep your thesis statement simple, and avoid using jargon.

- **Brown-nose.** All professors have their favorite ideas, concepts, and approaches, and they loved to be stroked. Try to work your prof's faves into the essay in any way possible.

- **Outline.** Once you have a thesis statement, outline the entire essay. This may take time, but it is to your benefit. When you are finished, turn the outline in with your exam because if you run out of time, you may get some credit for the outline. In outlining your essay, try this very simple structure:
   —Main point
   —Two details or examples
   —Two-sentence explanation of the examples
   —Restated main point

- **Get the most important info down first.** Once you have outlined the essay, begin the essay with your thesis statement. After that, put your most important ideas first. Often professors do not read the whole exam, only your topic sentences and evidence. As you write, don't worry about spelling and grammar, and don't think too hard; just bust through it. Write big, and use only one side of the paper. If you can, err on the side of too much information and too much explanation. More is better. Also, try to end your essay with a restatement of your thesis.

- **One more time.** If you have time, go back and review. Give it a good once-over for spelling and grammar first. If you have time, focus on rewriting your thesis for clarity; then move on to every main point statement and transition for every paragraph.

Under a worst-case scenario in which you don't finish the exam, write in the remainder of your outline and write that you ran out of time. If you find that you do not know the answer to the essay question at all, bullshit and write something. There is a chance that you may get some credit.

### Multiple Choice

The majority of tests that you will encounter in your college career will include some form of multiple choice questions. This is both a good and a bad thing. It is a bad thing because it is evidence of how uncreative the academy is, but it is also a good thing because multiple choice tests put the right answer in front of you every time. However, professors love to hide these answers and do so in a way that has the potential to be very difficult. They hide answers by tweaking details or using complicated language like double negatives. Your task is to wade through this petty intellectual subterfuge and get the goods:

- **Watch for modifiers.** Watch out for words like *not true* and *except*. A question worded like this makes you look for the wrong answer, which is counterintuitive. Bad, bad prof for the invention of this one.

- **Watch for absolutes.** Watch out for absolute words in answers: *never, none, always, all.* These are usually incorrect.
- **Read it through.** Read all choices before answering, and mark each with true, false, or nothing.
- **Consider all of the above.** If you have an option for "all of the above," see if any two options are correct. If so, "all of the above" is your answer. If one option is true and you are somewhat unsure about another, go with "all of the above." Statistically it is the correct answer more often than not.
- **Value sameness.** If two answers are very similar, home in on them. One of those is likely your boy.
- **Avoid extremes.** If an option is totally off base or absurd, ax it. If you are presented with a series of numbers or dates and are not sure of the right answer, ax the bottom and top one, and go with one in the middle.
- **The bigger, the better.** In a pinch, pick the most complete option—the one that has the most information.
- **Look for grammar.** If the stem (prompt) of the question is an incomplete sentence, make sure your answer forms a complete grammatically correct sentence. Answers that do not form grammatically correct sentences are wrong. Cross them off.

### Short Answers and Others of Its Kind

Any question that forces you to write out the correct answer is difficult. Short answer, identification, or fill in the blank requires you to recall the information, not just recognize it. For these types of questions, think about the following:

- **Gauge the length.** While reading the directions, think about whether you are being asked for a short definition or a more complete explanation. One thing to look at is the point breakdown. On a twenty-point test, a five-point question should have a complete answer.

- **Be to the point.** If you just have to give a definition, get it out as fast as possible; the idea is to try and get down the important words or concepts. When you are done, underline the words that you think are most important. If you are required to give a more complex answer, try this structure:

  —Main point

  —Three details, ideas, or explanations

  —Restated main point

### Matching Questions

The principle behind approaching matching questions is pretty straightforward. Here's what we do:

1. **Skim.** Skim all options in both columns, and try to look for a pattern. Ask yourself what it is testing—names and accomplishments, for example, or terms and definitions.

2. **One at a time.** Pick one column, and start with the first item. Cover up all the rest. Scan the opposite column from top to bottom, reading all of the options. Choose only after you have read *all* the options. Choose when you are pretty certain you have the right answer. If you have any doubt, skip it and move on.

Continue to do this until you have answered all those that you know for certain. Only then should you start to guess.

### True-False Questions

We like these the best because even if we don't remember our own name, the odds are in our favor that we will get these right. To up the odds even further on T/F questions, try the following:

- **Think true.** Go into each question thinking it is true and look for what is wrong with it.
- **Watch for modifiers.** Watch out for any modifier in the prompt. Most 100 percent statements, like, "All Irish men are large in stature," are false.
- **Watch for lists.** Watch out for any statement that has a long list of things. Look through that list carefully, and try to find one thing that is wrong. If you do, it gets the F.
- **Think logically.** Watch out for two true statements illogically joined. For example, "Dave is fat because the loft is dirty." Both are true but not causally linked.
- **Don't leave blanks.** Never leave a T/F blank, and when in doubt guess true. Statistically, true occurs more often than false.

That concludes the tips for true and false and for taking exams overall. Keep these in mind as the finals roll in, and remember: They are just a game, not who you are. In the last section, we look at one of the most powerful tools in our arsenal for playing the exam game and winning: interpreting our test results.

## SECTION 4: INTERPRETING TEST RESULTS

So, you have busted your ass to prep for your exams and have now learned how to master the exam game. Before we go any further, give yourself a huge pat on the back. You're doing a great job and should sit down and chill out. However, when you walk into class and get that blue exam book back with your grade, it is time to put the thinking cap back on. Reviewing an exam you have taken is a powerful tool for learning. We know this may be a terrifying prospect (throughout high school, Jon did not look at one grade he got back or any comments on any exam), but trust us, it is worth it. In this last section we look at how reexamining your exam will help you review more effectively in the future, become a better test taker, and (although we hate to admit it) help you learn the content of the course better. What follows is how to interpret your test results as a learning experience.

### Review Your Test; Study Better Next Time

Now it is time to figure out how to review more effectively next time. By going over your test, you can see what information needs to get more attention next time and where to get it. With test in hand, do the following:

- **Evaluate the structure.** Go through your test ignoring whether you got answers right or wrong. You are looking for the breakdown of your test—how it was structured and what information got the most points. Find a place to write this down. It is critical for shaping an effective review come next time. (See Chapter 8, "Cram Like a Pro.")
- **Evaluate the content.** Don't stress about right and wrong answers yet. Your goal here is to figure out where the question came from in the class (notes or lecture), what type of questions were asked (literal or analytical), and what type of information was tested (terms, theories, etc.). This stuff is gold for review.
- **Look at strengths.** It is good to know what worked in your review. Dive right into the questions you nailed, thinking about the type of material you know backward and forward and reminding yourself how you reviewed for that specific information.
- **Look at weaknesses.** With compassion, turn to the questions you got wrong. What type of information was it? Try to think why you got it wrong. Push beyond the "I just

didn't know it," to something more constructive, like, "I didn't know the answer because I forgot a detail." Focus specifically on mistakes in your reviewing methods; for example, you were only able to recognize information, not recall it.

- **Plan for the next time.** With all of this in mind, try to articulate what you would do differently next time for reviewing. Be constructive. What information would you focus more on? What organizational strategies would you use again and which ones are going out the window?

Always keep in mind that reviewing is a process. If this seems a little rough to you, however, know that professors almost always value improvement. If you go over your test, review better, and get a better grade on the next exam, your GPA will thank you.

### Reviewing to Test Better

Reviewing past exams, like an athlete watching a videotape of a past big game, can help you become a better test taker. What follows are some things to think about when it is time to reexamine your exam. In all of these, look for both strengths and weaknesses. Here is what to look for:

- **Get the big picture.** Review your test once over to get a sense of your performance as a whole. Pay close attention to sections (multiple choice, essay, short answer, etc.) you did well on and others that were dumpy, all the time looking for patterns. Next exam, remind yourself to spend more time on any sections you did drastically worse on. You may even want to write it on the top of your next exam: "Spend more time on . . ."
- **Look at your momentum.** While looking for patterns in your exam, also look for any trends in performance.

Look at how you started: Did you run out of steam at the end? If so, next exam, review the end of your exam closely, and try to bring some caffeine or food. Conversely, see if you took a while to warm up and didn't get going until the end. If so, remember to review the first half and also to do some warm-ups while waiting for the exam (freewriting and such). Also look to see if there were spikes in your performance—times when you were on and others when you were not. This may indicate that you need to take frequent breaks during the exam and review every five questions. Finally, note if you finished. If not, did you spend too much time on a particular question? Remember next time to force yourself to schedule your time.

- **Look at how it was graded.** This is relevant mostly for essay exams but a good thing to do in general. Did your prof give half-credit for attempted answers? If so, next exam show your work. In the essays, what kinds of information were valued? Where were the comments made? Try to figure out if all the professor read was the thesis, main points, and transitions. In the next exam, make sure these are clearly written and possibly underlined.

- **Find "stupid" mistakes.** All of us make these all the time, so don't be too hard on yourself. Stupid mistakes are things like missing a question, skipping a question inadvertently, not reading the directions, not finishing a question, or just a plain and simple, "I knew that." Going over your exam, try to figure out what type of stupid mistakes you made most often. On your next exam, at the top of the paper, write these mistakes down as a test review checklist.

- **Look at changed answers.** Some of us change for the better, and some of us change for the worse. If you discover you are the latter, write on the top of your exam, "Do not change answers unless totally positive."

You have just improved your next test score by at least ten points. Guaranteed. Our last thing to do with an old exam is use it for, of all things, pure and simple learning.

### Reviewing Your Exam to Learn

We hate to admit it, but your exam can teach you more about the content of the course. Also, for courses with final exams, reviewing your exams will get you better grades. Many final exams recycle questions—maybe not verbatim, but pretty damn close. With your test in hand, here is what to do:

- **Take test notes.** Final exams often recycle questions, so taking careful notes on the content of your exam can help at the end of the semester. You can take these notes however you like, but try to have one central space to hold all the information you get from your review. Keep it to one page, and stick it in your notebook.
- **Break down wrong answers.** As always, go back into your test with compassion. Once you find a legitimate mistake, not a "stupid" mistake, figure out exactly what the question was testing. If applicable, figure out the broadest category it tested. For example, if you got a case study about a woman who was afraid to leave her house, you would identify that that question was testing you on agoraphobia. Next, think over your course, and identify where this question came from. If it came from your textbook, which chapter? If lecture, which day?
- **Go get the answer.** It is time to go get the answer. Approach the question not as a wrong answer but as a problem, and go back into your notes and textbook to find the answer (see "Reading Like Einstein," page 151). When you find the solution, read the surrounding material and solve the problem, paying close attention to what you did

not know or apply the first time around. On your note sheet, record what you learned by solving the problem.

- **Take queries to the prof.** Look for questions you think were wrongly graded. After reading the question over, go back into your various sources and get evidence to prove you are correct. If you still believe you are in the right, go to the professor. The best approach here is to disagree calmly with the grade (throwing a fit and ranting, although cathartic, does no good), and present your argument in a rational way. After you are done presenting your case, listen to the professor's response. If he or she is cool, the prof will explain why he or she is either changing or not changing your grade, a win-win situation. Even if the grade is not changed, you still have learned about the topic in question by formulating an argument and then listening to your professor's response.

That concludes learning from your exams, and that concludes playing the exam game and winning. All done.

## SUMMARY

Just when you think you are out, we pull you back. There is always a summary. But this one is easy. Seeing how you just mastered the exam game, let's try a little test to review:

**The Question.** Exams are:

a. stupid.
b. a mediocre means to evaluate understanding of content.
c. A game that can mastered and beaten.
d. All of the above.

You know that answer. Test well, be well, and remember, exams are just a game.

# Part III:  Beyond Beating the System

# 10: Living a Life
# Less Ordinary

On August 12, 1998, we found ourselves together at Landmark College in Putney, Vermont, working on what would eventually become this book. It was almost a year since we had first met at transfer orientation and sat nervously around a circle. We arrived at Brown as two kids determined to make peace with the past by finding academic success. And we did just that, in spades. And so we began writing this book, going back over our past and coming to terms with the personal ramifications of our academic success.

A year after transferring, we realized that we had worked hard to heal our past with academic success, but deep inside we knew better than anyone else that our worth and intelligence were not synonymous with the narrow standards by which academic performance is measured. School develops and values less than 10 percent of what it means to be human and to live a full life. Learning outside the lines and living a life less ordinary is about moving beyond blackboards and academic success, to creating experiences that embrace and nurture the parts of our selves that are left unrealized by traditional education.

We began this journey with the stories of two kids who grew up on the outside looking in. Our study skills were the tools that freed us from our past and opened the doors to our future, but our performance in school was never, and will never be, who we are. So now we set the study skills aside and open a new chapter in our lives. We return to how to find personal empowerment outside school and how to obtain true academic success by creating new learning environments. Finally, we look at the concept of living a life less ordinary, the most revolutionary concept of all.


## SECTION 1: SAVING THE SELF FROM THE INSTITUTION

We have talked a lot about the impact that pursuing the ideal of normalcy had on our learning, but we have not yet fully explored the emotional ramifications. When you accept the definition of normal that is imposed by the institution, you become alienated from yourself. There is a vast and unspoken emotional wasteland that sits at the clay feet of the academic heights we so ambitiously scale. Jon experienced it after climbing those heights at both LMU and Brown, but looked down only to see emptiness inside him. The striving for success whittled away at Jon's sense of self, as it does to thousands of children every day. We addressed this theme in Chapter 3, but it keeps coming back because it is at the core of the book, and is key to what it means to learn outside the lines. The most destructive power of education is that it devalues intuitiveness and originality. College is no exception.

Although higher education holds high ideals about personal discovery and intellectual development, there is still a bitter pragmatic reality we must face. How can we ignore the fact that college is a professional track, and it is rare that we are encouraged to look inward to define who we are or what we want, or chart an individualized path. Success becomes external, in markers like the GPA, internships, and the networking we do.

It is not much different from the simplistic way elementary school teachers understand intelligence. It is easier this way, never looking inward to see that each individual has a different path he or she might take. There are no two roads to success that are identical, just as there are no two minds that are the same. We battled deeply with this issue of personal conformity, as intensely as we did with academic conformity. It takes courage to stake a claim to your identity.

Defining success and happiness for yourself is a victory. In the end, it is your life, and how you define success and happiness is your call. The point is to engage with this struggle. What follows are some concrete steps we took to take back ourselves from the institution.

### Developing the Reflective Self—Traveling the Road to Emotional Clarity

Yes, this section is loosely about mental health, and, yes, we are both about as nutty as a bar in the West Village on a Thursday night. And that is okay because we have no desire to become normal, thank you. In fact, we are traveling the road to emotional clarity from the polar opposite perspective.

The act of self-reflection is an act of defiance. We are not taught to look inward for guidance, but outward to our academic "success" for approval and acceptance. In spite of our personal psychoses, we know that actively dealing with our own mental health, regardless of how far we have yet to go, has made a great difference in our lives.

Here are some ideas to help you through this process:

- **Think about getting shrunk.** Shrink Head has played a huge role in our lives. If it were up to us, we'd have Shrink Head's picture on the front of this book. Engaging with Shrink Head may or may not be right for you. But our point is this: there is no shame if it works for you. It is most difficult to make the commitment to grow as a person. Doing so is honorable and worthwhile.

- **Ask hard questions.** What are your goals? Whom are you pleasing? Whose expectations are you trying to meet? How do you feel when you are in school? Where does that little kid hide, and when does he or she come out? These are the hard questions that most people are too afraid to ask. But we are not like most other people, and neither are you.

- **Be spiritual.** We are not concerned with answering the big question, Is there a God? right this minute. That is up to you. Our point is that there is a time in all of our lives to give some thought to what you believe in outside yourself, whether it is meditation, Christianity, Judaism, Islam, or something else. Searching for your spirituality is an intensely personal act, but one that will ultimately connect you to things greater than yourself. Have faith.

- **Pursue balance.** We take the hypocrite award for this little tip. But despite our workaholic tendencies and compulsiveness, it is a good thing to pursue a balanced life. Take it from us: our lives were not meant to be spent doing only work. Find things you love to do that have nothing to do with achievement, take time off, sleep in, and, most important, try to be in the moment. Working is an end, not an identity in and of itself.

- **Know and trust your gut.** For some amazing reason, we all have a little voice somewhere deep down inside that knows what is right for ourselves. But this voice gets covered up by years of believing that the intuitive self is stupid compared to the rational, logical mind. To get to the intuitive self, we have to put the logical mind in its place. A good way to do this is to try to home in on first reactions—the stuff that comes right to the mind or gut—before you start thinking. Practice watching for and feeling this first reaction. You'll get to know your gut this way, and ultimately be able to listen to your better self.

### Developing the Creative and Passionate Self

Too often, creativity and passion, two of the best things about being alive, get pushed out of our definition of self. Creativity is often restricted to art, when in fact it is a way of engaging with the world, a way of thinking and living. In fact, the imagination is the root of all change, because it allows us to imagine a world different from the one we live in. Pursuing creative endeavors, whether sculpting or writing essays, allows us to live fully in the world, drawing on our emotions, our personality, our intelligence, and our souls. Creativity is not concerned with solutions in a logical linear sense, but rather embraces the ironies, complexities, and humanity in our daily lives.

In a world concerned with normalcy, the passionate self also gets the boot. Passion is threatening, and when we live with gusto, we take huge risks by rocking the boat. But a passion for things, for people, for ideas, is what we are all looking for, what this business of success is all about. Keep on the lookout for activities, classes, or the like that arouse your passion. These are the kinds of activities that when you start them, the restrictions placed on you fall away, and your life becomes like flying. You're gone, without knowing it and without having any control.

When you experience these times and have clicked into the zone, try to remember what you were doing. Were you creating art, working with kids, reading, writing, or simply going for a walk and thinking about the buildings along the way. Write these times down, or record them in whatever form works for you. We spend only about 5 percent of our lives succeeding and about 5 percent failing. The rest churns and tumbles in an inevitable but ultimately human process.

Too often, in our schools and in our higher education, being a creative, passionate person is considered extracurricular. We had to fight to integrate passion and creativity into our lives. Although this is one of the most individualized of the topics in this chapter, here are tangible things to think about to bring out your creative and passionate self:

- **Be with children.** No one on the planet is more creative and passionate than kids. Their joy for life and creative way of moving in the world are contagious. Spend time with them, hold them, and talk with them. They will teach you more about love, creativity, and passion than any professor, textbook, or self-help manual ever could.
- **Be involved in the world.** Newspapers, magazines, even strangers on the street are all easy entry points to this complicated drama. Engage with this complexity, read the paper, get pissed off when protesters are gassed, be sad when children bring guns to school, and rejoice in the victories on athletic fields. This is the good stuff. Passion has no judgment and no IQ.
- **Journal, sketch, and record.** Create a space in which you can record and keep the things you see about yourself, such as how you engage with the world and what you are thinking about. Do it however you want, just so that it works for your mind. Some suggestions are: nightly journal entries (just let it go; don't stress about communicating in any coherent way or spelling and grammar); sketching in a sketchbook; or recording your thoughts with a tape recorder.
- **Seek out popular culture.** Blow homework off. Listen to music, go to a play, or watch a movie. The creative arts, especially music, are powerful. Music cuts through all the bullshit; it is not about language, ideas, or arguments but about emotions. For us, music has played a healing role. There is more value in these activities than in a week of homework.

- **Make things.** We don't mean make art. The creative mind
  is so much more than art. What we mean is to spend part
  of your time creating plays, art, music, or models for public service programs. Don't ever listen to anyone who tells
  you that you are not qualified to make things. These are
  stupid linear people caught in the rat race we're trying to
  get out of.

### Developing the Connected Self

All of us feel the pressure to deny the parts of ourselves that
do not fit in. In response to that pressure, we abandon our
friends, our communities, our families. But connection to
these people and places is far more important than GPAs.
Moreover, being connected to where you come from, whether
it is a dyslexic household like Jon's, the inner city, or the Mid-
west, is a powerful life experience. Connection to your roots
grounds you and affirms the intuitive self. And in the end, our
relationships are all we ever keep and all we ever really have.
We don't know your life, your history, but here are some things
we have done in our lives to stay connected to our families, our
communities, and our friends:

- **Know your family history.** Much of academic success is
  about doing better than the prior generation and about
  changing things that do not enable us to fit in. Screw that.
  Families—their history, their unique complexities—are
  the most exciting stuff around. It is where you get your
  character, your personality. God knows we had our share
  of dysfunctional family events, and we have our skeletons
  buried deep in the family storage. But, like us, you should
  spend time knowing where you come from, where your
  folks come from, and, if applicable, what your siblings'

lives are like. Talk with them; our family past holds much of the future.

- **Call home once a week.** The Sunday phone call (just a random day) has done wonders for our relationships with the folks. Try it. You'll feel more grounded, even if you brawl with them on the phone.
- **Get political.** All communities have issues. Take a stand; get involved; do public service; read about the history of your community. Pursue change for the things you believe in for your community.
- **Seek challenging relationships.** We go with the less-is-more philosophy when it comes to friends. Seek out those people who challenge you to grow as a person. Most important, stay with friends who are committed to the relationship, who are there for you in times of struggle as well as times of success. If you find people like this, and they are rare, hold on to them and keep in touch. They ground you to what is important and are powerful life-changing connections.

### Developing the Resilient Self

The resilient self is what we are striving to create and striving to be. This is the warrior in all of us. For us, it developed over years of fighting for our identities in schools, surrounded by families who fought side by side with us. In the end, this is who we are. But often in the struggle to survive in school, we forget how to forge our own path and how to rock the boat like the little kid who will not sit at his desk but demands an explanation of why he should.

Learning outside the lines and living a life less ordinary are about being a warrior and telling "them" to screw their gold stars and template identities. It would be ironic if we attempted to tell you how to do this. We can't; we wouldn't even dare. But here are some things to think about to help develop the warrior inside you:

- **Personally define success.** You own your definition of success. In your own life, define what it means to *you*, not others, to be successful.
- **Find the fan club.** Try to identify people in your life who can celebrate your successes with you. Sometimes the best people to do this are people who have been there since the very beginning. When something good comes up, fax that paper to them, or call them on the phone.
- **Survive setbacks.** Setbacks suck. No further analysis necessary. Worse still, they are a fact of life. The short version is that setbacks are like acid flashbacks, ushering in fears and doubts in our abilities. When setbacks come rolling in—and they will if you are rocking the boat— relax, take a deep breath, and know that they are the inevitable by-product of working hard and taking risks. If you don't have setbacks, you're not trying hard enough. For more tips, see the Surviving Setbacks box.

---

### SURVIVING SETBACKS

1. **Get perspective:**
   - Look at successes: prior good grades, personal success.
   - Talk to someone about the problem.
   - Look outside academics for success.

2. **Do something:**
   - Do anything that is task related.
   - Ask for help in ascertaining the next step.

3. **Suit up and show up:**
   - Go to class.
   - Shower.
   - Eat.
   - Talk to your professor.

4. **Get refreshed:**
   - Exercise.
   - Meditate.
   - Take a walk.

- **Embrace struggle and risk.** These are two big ones we were taught to shy away from, but, in fact, they are key to becoming empowered individuals. Too many people define happiness as euphoria and so try to avoid struggle. And risk brings up the fear of failure we all are taught to run from. But there is meaning in the struggle, and only by taking risks will we grow and find success.
- **Don't fear failure.** We grow up fearing the big "F-word." When we get F's, we do not get the gold stars, right? But the irony is that without risking failure, we will never achieve anything that is truly ours. Committing yourself to living a life on your own terms and pursuing your own goals and definition of success are risky. Know in the back of your mind that the resilient part of yourself is strong, and your identity is independent of your performance or success. When looked at in this light and without fear, failure simply becomes an exciting but meaningless game of poker.

On last piece of advice: Taking back the self from the institution of education is a lifelong struggle, but is also a life lesson. Through everything we do, our careers, our relationships, and institutions of all kinds impose values on us. The ideas in this section—staying connected, finding your passion, and being a warrior in everything you do—will change your life and help you stay true to yourself.

Now that we have saved the self from the institution, we are on to the search for new ways to learn. In this section, we explore the power of alternative ways to learn within and outside the institution of education.

## Section 2: True Academic Success and the Search for New Ways to Learn

How often have you been in lecture and felt that you were only scratching the surface of a subject and that your mind needed more than logical, linear, scientific intelligence? During our years at Brown, we also encountered a learning environment too limited and too narrow for the multifaceted way our minds process information. But we sat in lecture, read the textbooks, and took the rote exams over and over again, always watching our education pass us by.

Regardless of how self-directed we are or grow to be in our learning, we cannot get around the reality that school is fundamentally a narrow learning environment. Even in one of the most progressive universities in the county, we found the same elementary school infrastructure, a classroom filled with different types of learners, and one teacher. And like elementary school, the only institutional means for any type of individualized education is DSS.

Some people assume that the university is the best environment to learn in. We wasted much of our time believing that there was only one environment, the classroom, that facilitated "true" learning. But in fact, true learning cannot and should not ever be held prisoner by the classroom. The point of academic success is not to take at face value the rhetoric of institutions but to challenge what is assumed to be true every step of the way.

There are more powerful environments to learn in than the classroom and lecture hall. Moving beyond the classroom to redefine academic success and search for a new learning environment is a powerful step toward self-empowerment and getting the most out of education. In this section, we explore how to individualize your education within the environment of the university. Then we present an alternative learning paradigm: the power of learning by doing.

### Individualizing Your Education

An individualized education is truly the means to academic success, but very few institutions hold this as a core value or are equipped to pull it off (Oxford is the only one that comes to mind). But we keep trying it anyway. In face of the limitations of most universities, here are some strategies we have used in our academic career to individualize our education:

- **Know yourself.** The first step toward an individualized education is internal. Knowing how you learn, what type of mind you have, opens up new environments for you. This type of self-knowledge will tell you what courses to avoid and what to fill your schedule with. This is a personal journey. Think back over your life, looking to identify when you learned best. Focus not on grades but on when you loved learning. Stay with this memory, and see what it brings up.

- **Use the power of relationships.** We talk about the power of connections in Chapter 3, but this is when it really comes into play. If you develop a personal relationship with your teacher and you know how you learn, you can create a tremendous opportunity for yourself. If you find yourself in a relationship with a professor, try to push the scope of your learning environment. For example, we have a friend at Brown who made an agreement to do all of his tests as essays, although the rest of the class took multiple choice. You can also try doing research with your professor as a means to individualize your work. The bottom line is to use your relationships to learn more dynamically.

- **Independent study.** This is the best way to individualize your education. All schools and all majors have them. The trick is to find a professor who is willing to work with you and whose work you respect. Design a class, pitch it, and you're off. Nothing is more self-directed or individualized than this.
- **The independent major.** A close second to independent study, independent majors allow you to individualize your course of study. Most schools have these, and they allow you essentially to design a major. This is a pain in the ass most of the time, but if you have an idea, go with it.

If you decide to pursue any or all of the above, know that you are engaging in a radical notion of education, one that is revolutionary. This is your education, and you have a right to one that respects your individuality.

### Project-Based Learning

This is the big one, the learning environment to beat all learning environments. Project-based learning or experiential learning is rooted in the fact that the act of *doing* in a focused manner uses numerous multimodal ways of learning. The power of doing as a learning experience is not just skill oriented but also an effective way to learn content, modes of thought, and models of communication. Evidence for the power of this type of learning is all around us and pretty easy to find. Look no further than your childhood. How do children learn? They touch, they crawl, they move, they fall down, they hear, they experience the world.

But the power of experience is making a comeback, and now the headlines are touting the power of doing in mainstream elementary education reform. Not that this notion of learning by doing is anything new. John Dewey, one of the foremost educational theorists, believed strongly in the power of doing. If you don't trust the academics (we don't blame you for that), just check out the coveted professional degrees. The highest levels of the most competitive types of advanced education and professional training embrace the power of doing as learning. For student doctors, the vast majority of training occurs through internship and residency. Beyond that, many of the top medical schools have adopted a case study curriculum as the primary means of pedagogy.

Project-based learning is a legitimate and powerful learning experience. The problem is that no one has figured out how to institutionalize experiential learning. On one hand, this makes sense. Experiential learning by definition is something that escapes institutionalization. But there is an antagonism toward this type of learning. The academy is dominated by a logical and scientific mode of thought that looks down on this type of learning. That means we have to find it ourselves.

The fact is that the projects we have undertaken had a more profound impact on our lives and our learning than any course. You are reading one of those projects right now. Writing this book taught us more about our minds, ourselves, and our weaknesses than we ever wanted to know, and we learned more about writing and education than two master's degrees put together. Also, and we get to this in more detail in the epilogue, a service project called Eye-to-Eye runs a close second to the book as a huge experiential learning environment. This projects works with LD/ADHD children, and simply walking the halls of the elementary school the first day of the program packed in enough "learning" for us to earn a graduate degree in special education and psychology.

Most important, beyond the content or skills learned, we were profoundly affected by our experience with project-based learning. These experiences changed who we are, and they changed our lives. How often can we say that about information given in a lecture? We lived those ideas and skills; we experienced them and integrated them into our lives.

When you read something, you retain 20 percent of the information; when you read it and say it out loud, you retain 35 percent; and when you read, speak, and review it, you retain 50 percent. But when you experience it and make it part of your life, in the end it is truly yours. It is too bad that more universities have not committed themselves to giving their students access to such a powerful experience.

We apologize for planting these seeds in your mind and not having many answers about how to get it in your life. However, we do have some suggestions that may help if you decide to create this experience for yourself:

- **Bring your life into your work.** Although project-based learning cannot be institutionalized, the thing about it is that you cannot escape it. It is everywhere, all the time, and in everything you do. One of the ways to access this is to be self-reflective. Explore your life—where you come from, what you've been through—and then bring it into your academic work however you can. This may mean choosing a specific major, or it may mean using your life experiences for papers. Too often we are taught that our life and our academics are separate. They are not.
- **Do it in the classroom.** This is a positive outcome of pursuing an individualized education through personal relationships. If you develop a relationship with a professor, you can push the boundaries of how you learn in the class. Try designing an alternative project with your professor to

replace a test or paper. We've done this in the past, and so have our friends. It gets good grades and is better learning. Not much more than you can ask for.

- **Explore service-learning.** This is a new and exciting concept that is similar to our experience with Project Eye-to-Eye. In a developing trend in colleges across the country, many courses integrate service into the curriculum. To find these classes, go to the service center on campus, or search on-line the course announcement of "service-learning." If your campus does not have any service-learning courses, do service on your own, a powerful way to get "doing" involved in your academics.

- **Seek out "doing" classes.** Some classes embrace doing more than others. Traditional creative arts classes, writing classes, and visual arts classes are all focused on the act of producing work. Also, many science classes, classes like speech, and some business or other professional classes are focused around practical application of what is learned.

- **Make things.** To learn by doing, the best thing to do is make stuff. That's all we can tell you. Make whatever you want: a sculpture, a poem, a service project. Just make stuff. You will learn, feel good, and feel alive.

- **Be open.** Watch for the experiences that may come your way, and when the opportunity arises, take it. Have no fear. Experience holds more knowledge than a thousand academics or textbooks.

Having searched for new learning environments, we are now on to the concluding section of this book. We look at how our journey thus far—the study skills, developing ourselves, and searching for new learning environments—is applicable to living a life less ordinary.

## SECTION 3: LIVING A LIFE LESS ORDINARY

We are quickly approaching the end: the end of this section, the end of the chapter, and, yep, the end of our book. But this is okay with us, because this ending, like all other endings, opens a new chapter in all of our lives. This book is about freeing ourselves from a past scarred by an institution that is the gatekeeper to our futures, our identities, and our sense of self and well-being. At its core, this book is about using our education to free our selves.

Part II, "Schooled," outlined tools for you to find success within the institution for personal, pragmatic, and political reasons, all of which you defined for yourself. The study skills were also about demystifying the institution of education, opening up our schools' narrow halls to alternative learning. Ultimately, these skills were about empowering you to individualize your education in a revolutionary way.

And now we move past the academic battle, to explore how to win a much more significant war. We come back to what was with us in the halls of elementary school, hiding with us in the bathroom, and what brought us to Brown. Our entire lives we have fought against living ordinary lives, ones that define us by our gold stars. We have always fought to live passionate lives, trying to get back to that little foul-mouthed redhead and the little ball of energy who did not care what other people thought about them. And so we come back to the purpose of this book. Learning outside the lines is about living a life less ordinary—about living a beautiful life that is truly yours.

But guess what? We are all on our own for this one. This is your life. What do you want to do with it? We have one last fleeting piece of advice: Do differently. The challenge of living an individualized, empowered, and creative life is a challenge that faces all of us.

So what do you want to do now? Maybe go run naked

through your campus, write frantic letters, read poetry, drive to New Orleans to buy a used car, ride the Amtrak trains for the hell of it, take time off, make art, be an investment banker, if that is it for you. Do something that is truly yours. No matter how absurd your venture may seem, or how creative or off-beat, no matter how many times you hear it is going to fail, or how many times you hear that you should have "reasonable expectations," remember that you are not alone in your desire to live a life less ordinary.

What do we do now that we are winding down the book? We go back to our lives, whether it is school, work, or simply figuring out what our lives should be and who the hell we are. But we go back knowing that the past does not determine our future. We go back now keeping our struggle close to our heart, and wearing our victories on our sleeves, and never forgetting where we came from. Our struggles make us stronger, and our wounds heal and knit together to constitute the strength of the fabric of our character. No one can ever take that away from us. It takes courage to fight against a deep-seated and unquestioned oppression. We are all greater than the gold stars, the report cards, and any limitations put on us. Go back to your life, and have faith in who and what you are.

When you face oppression and an institution that attempts to define you by its terms, remember who we all are. There is an English major out there who spells at a third-grade level; he wrote this book. Remember the kid who lived in the detention room, a high school dropout, a drug addict; he wrote this book.

But things like scaling the walls of the Ivy Tower are only stepping-stones. The true victory is that we all continue to struggle and continue to fight for life outside of institutions, a life that is inside ourselves—a connected, passionate, creative, and beautiful life. When our report cards fade from our memory and we have healed the wounds from our past, and when college rankings and our GPA bleed into oblivion, what stays is a beautiful and profound struggle to be true to ourselves that no one, not even time, can ever take away from us.

# Epilogue: Project Eye-to-Eye

On January 27, 2000, after turning in the final draft of this book and sleeping off a stress-induced caffeine-saturated fog, we faced the next big project of our lives: what to do after graduation (beside the book-signing tour). That decision was quite possibly the only thing more frightening than writing down our past.

When we finished the book and embraced the challenge of graduation, we eventually came back to the same place we ended: doing it differently. This chapter shows you how we walked our talk and stayed true to ourselves despite a deluge of corporate recruiting and the pressure toward graduate or professional school and how we are trying to find a way to live a life less ordinary.

So for our parting shot of all parting shots, we are going to tell you about our future, about Project Eye-to-Eye, a program that takes university students with LD/ADHD and matches them up with elementary school children with similar learning profiles. This program is our passion, contains our soul, and is our route to a future less ordinary.

Enjoy and remember: this is our individualized attempt to be true to ourselves. However, the program's core principles are timeless and universal. As always, the core values of this program are about becoming empowered individuals and not spinning the wheels of the rat race round and round.

PROJECT EYE-TO-EYE: SOMETHING VERY SPECIAL

There are over thirty million people in the United States with LD/ADHD who think like us, the vast majority with an average or above-average IQ. Only 1.8 percent of these people will go on to a four-year college education, and only 5 percent will go on to any form of higher education. One in five children will be diagnosed with a reading disability or attention disorder, and over 60 percent of these children will never graduate from high school.

For us, our "doing" was to create a program designed to help kids who think as we do and are now struggling much as we did. From these horrific statistics, from our experience, and from our guts, grew Project Eye-to-Eye. In the beginning, Eye-to-Eye was only a small public service project in Providence. In just a year, it grew into a nationally recognized intervention program, the only one of its kind in the country. Today, it is a nonprofit organization in New York; Jonathan is the executive director, and David is a part-time artistic consultant.

It all began in Room 4 at the Fox Point School in Providence.

### Room 4: Gifted Is As Gifted Does

On March 22, 1998, we and a group of LD/ADHD students from Brown watched with trepidation as the blue linoleum floors of Fox Point Elementary School passed under our feet. We were heading toward Room 4.

All we had in our hands was a box of junk, four glue guns, and some tile panels. As we walked in, the heads from the circle turned abruptly toward us with looks of anxious and skeptical anticipation. As we waited to begin, kids from the other after-school clubs wanted to come inside, but only Eye-to-Eye kids were allowed to take part.

The room moved with a nervous and hyperactive energy as one by one we fidgeted, our attention waxed and waned, and the handwriting on the board became illegible and misspelled. We all laughed. We started with the mentors first: "My name is Kent. I have ADHD. Strengths, well, ah, ah, I got 1600 on my SATs. Weakness, well, ah, ah, I have a really hard time paying attention."

"My name is Dave. I am really good at working with my hands. I made my first metal sculpture when I was four. I have a hard time paying attention too, and it's hard for me to sit still."

"My name's Dave. I love music and I am really good with people. Reading's really hard for me. I used to have to go outside when I was in elementary school all by myself during reading class because I was so bad. It made me feel stupid."

As each Brown student spoke of struggles and successes, the kids shouted out, "That's like me." And then, no more talking, just doing. The junk spilled out on the floor, and each adult-kid pair split off to work on a project. It was the first day. We have come to know better since then, but our expectations were too low for the kids we had in the room that day.

The project was a simple one-dimensional collage without a theme. We circled the room, each pair working, chatting, and then we stopped. In front of us was a three-dimensional collage of a landscape filled with animal crackers from our snack. Visually and conceptually, the collage was far beyond this grade level. We looked around the room. Everyone was doing stuff far beyond our expectations. Kids were making art about themes—about how it felt to be in school and about themselves. We had supposedly the "worst" and most at-risk kids in the school in our classroom. We had supposedly the most at-risk college students in the room. But suddenly those terms weren't relevant to any of us anymore.

The blue linoleum passed by much more easily for all of us mentors on the way out of the school that day. Going to the school and working with the kids had laid to rest some of our own demons. Most important, the work we did touched our kids. One of our kids with ADHD—the boy who had made the collage with animal crackers, a boy in third grade who lives in a special ed room where his peers are children with mental retardation and who has a clinical school phobia—left that day so excited to come back to school the next day that he couldn't sleep that night. All because we shared our stories, we were ourselves, and we cared.

Project Eye-to-Eye was born.

---

## THE CLAN

About two months before Eye-to-Eye began in the fall of 1998, we received a word of advice from a well-known published LD/ADHD professional. As well intentioned as she may have been, on hearing about the idea for Eye-to-Eye, she responded by saying, "That's a great idea if you can make it work. You *are* dealing with *LD/ADHD college students,* you know." She had obviously passed Deficit Model 305 (the advanced course) in that silly place they call Education Graduate School with flying colors. Professionals: you can't live with them, but you can't kill them.

Our program owes its success entirely to the LD/ADHD students and kids who constitute it. Soon enough, all of them will end up on those lists you see of famous LD/ADHD people. We pale in comparison and have been honored to work with them.

---

### The Mission and the Structure

Project Eye-to-Eye's mission is to empower the LD/ADHD community by challenging the pathological social and institutional ideology that surrounds LD/ADHD. Our method is to bring LD/ADHD college students into the lives of LD/ADHD elementary school students as role models, tutors, and mentors.

Each pair works approximately two to three hours a week in

the classroom during class in both so-called mainstreamed-integrated classrooms and special education classrooms. Beyond the classroom, all the pairs meet once a week for the Eye-to-Eye After School Club, where they work on art projects.

### *The Guiding Principles*

In developing Project Eye-to-Eye we have been guided by these principles of practice:

1. **Models of Success.** Project Eye-to-Eye is firmly rooted in the principle that LD/ADHD college students, regardless of where they go to school or their GPAs, are models of success. The program is based on our experience of struggle and success, and is rooted in the strengths and gifts we have to share with children who think like we do.

2. **Early Intervention with Long-Term Commitment.** Project Eye-to-Eye begins working with children as early as the second grade, and makes a commitment to pair them with a mentor until they graduate from ninth grade. It has been shown statistically that intervention is most effective with children at an early age. In our own lives, by the time we reached eighth grade, we were shut off from learning, our self-esteem shattered by our experience in elementary school. Most LD/ADHD children drop out after eighth grade. We believe in working with children all the way through this critical period of identity formation and development.

3. **Art as Learning and Empowerment.** Project Eye-to-Eye believes in art as a legitimate and powerful medium for learning abstract thinking skills, spatial relationships, and interpersonal skills. Through an artistic medium, Eye-to-Eye children are given an opportunity to access their gift for project-based, spatial, tactile and kinetic, and interpersonal learning within an academic environment. This experience helps them de-

velop their strengths and validates the unique gifts that are too often ignored within a traditional educational paradigm.

4. **All Kinds of Minds.** Project Eye-to-Eye believes that LD/ADHD children are not pathological aberrations but in fact are gifted alternative thinkers. We adhere to the principles of multiple intelligences and are committed to identifying and supporting alternative learning styles in all our children.

5. **Individualization.** Project Eye-to-Eye believes in the power of individualized education, yet also recognizes the financial limitations placed on schools. Our mentors' time, volunteered in the classroom, is invaluable in helping children to create a learner-centered learning environment. Armed with experience and rigorous professional training, our mentors work with classroom teachers to meet the needs of our kids. We work with schools to make the classroom environment and the presentation of information as accessible as it can be for the unconventional needs of our students.

6. **Collaboration/Partnership.** Project Eye-to-Eye believes in building a sustainable partnership with a local community school. We work together to share information, learn from others' experiences, and collaboratively solve problems.

7. **Empowerment Through Service.** Project Eye-to-Eye believes in creating community through empowerment and empowerment through service. The act of service is fundamentally empowering; the core principle of Eye-to-Eye is that we have something to give. As a result of our common purpose, a strong community has grown within the LD/ADHD population at Brown, supporting the development of friendships and creating a powerful learning environment for everyone involved.

8. **Empowerment as Activism.** As an empowered and active service community, we are changing negative perceptions of LD/ADHD by being in schools, being open about our experiences, and supporting the Eye-to-Eye kids.

### *The Project Eye-to-Eye Club: Art Is Not for Art's Sake*

Beyond the walls of the classroom, we focus on the strengths and alternative learning styles of our kids. This is a time and a space we never had as kids. Most of the time, art was either something extra to be done after the math homework or special projects that were for the "good" and "smart" kids with perfect grades. In the Project Eye-to-Eye After School Club, we use art to create an alternative learning environment that rewards our kids' gifts, while facilitating invaluable personal learning and skill development that is directly applicable to school.

The deficit model does not exist in this room. For the first time, our kids are in a space where LD/ADHD is the majority. In our room, they see Brown students, who have reached the highest levels of academic success, fidget uncontrollably with hyperactive energy and misspell the simplest of words.

Why art? Art is fundamentally a medium that requires creativity, logical thought, and abstract reasoning skills. Moreover, as a tool for learning, art allows LD/ADHD kids to use their tactile and kinetic and their spatial skills to find success. Finding success through their strengths is an opportunity rarely afforded our kids within the narrow parameters of the classroom.

What type of stuff do we make? Anything. To meet our goal of creating a challenging and stimulating environment, we push beyond traditional art projects toward more advanced mediums and concepts; our kids are far too advanced for macaroni and glitter art. Our projects are systematic and highly structured, and the goals are clearly articulated. Our structure for each day is: the sharing, the project, and the critique. In every project, we adhere to the following principles:

- **Safe from failure.** All of our art projects are failure proof. The key to failure-proof art is that our materials are cool.

Whether it is junk, toy soldiers, or something else, the goal is to get stuff that if you just put on a pedestal, it would look good, so nobody can fail. Each project has a discernible beginning, a middle, and an end, ensuring that when the time runs out, we have a finished-looking product.

- **Modeling.** In this environment, modeling occurs on two levels. First, mentors model personal, intellectual, and academic skills. Second, our mentors model an acceptance of self. Whether it is poor handwriting or fidgeting, our mentors provide the powerful message to our kids that it is a positive thing to accept what one cannot change. Acceptance of ourselves and of qualities we were taught to abhor is powerful for LD/ADHD kids to see.
- **Help required.** In all of our projects, getting help is how to do the project correctly. The message is clear: we all get help, all the time, and there is absolutely nothing wrong with that.
- **Process oriented.** All of the projects are broken down into their smallest parts—a beginning, a middle, and an end. This makes it safe from failure and also models the skill of micro-uniting, an invaluable skill for LD/ADHD students to refine.
- **Push beyond the comfort zone.** In everything we do, we push our personal boundaries, incorporating and modeling more advanced critical thinking skills. The goal is to keep challenging ourselves to think more creatively and to facilitate the development of the same skills in our children.

Using this structure for an hour and a half each week, all of us involved got a glimpse at how subjective, and wrong, the deficit model for LD/ADHD really is. In Room 4, in an empowering environment that embraces our gifts and accepts differences as the norm, we and our kids became the gifted ones in the school.

The deficit model is nowhere to be found.


STEPPING BACK

Leaving that day from Room 4, we were struck by the irony of the entire situation: ten Brown students with ADHD/LD, one who did not learn to read until he was twelve, another a high school dropout, standing in the middle of the special education room at Fox Point School. We had come full circle. But standing in Room 4 that day, after a year spent beating the system and launching Eye-to-Eye, we were fundamentally different people, no longer those little kids who in their heart of hearts believed they were stupid and crazy.

### *Eye-to-Eye as Solution, Empowerment, and Closure*

In Eye-to-Eye we created a learning environment that truly embraced our minds. We created solutions to broad social problems confronting LD/ADHD students. We empowered ourselves by the act of service. And finally, as empowered individuals, we shattered the deficit model.

### *Eye-to-Eye as an Alternative Learning Paradigm*

Our experience with Eye-to-Eye has allowed us to push the boundaries of our education. Eye-to-Eye became an alternative education environment that allowed us to progress beyond the paradigm of teacher-centered classroom learning and into project-based and experiential learning. As a learning environment, the experience of Eye-to-Eye is the pedagogy, and the lessons learned are the experience.

Like a chemical reaction, we arranged a series of elements

and then set them in motion with a catalyst, the sum total greater than its parts, but contingent on all the parts working together. The doing, the arrangement of the parts, the setting in motion, and then the motion itself was the learning environment for us, engaging and using the full gamut of our intelligence and our alternative learning styles.

The big question is, What did we learn? Did we learn skills? Did we learn about LD/ADHD? Did we learn how to teach? Did we learn about ourselves and our lives? Did we learn how to write? How to run meetings? How to develop a business proposal? How to think systemically about social problems? Did we learn how to work with people? Did we learn about our own limitations, strengths, and gifts? Did we learn about ourselves? And did we learn the value of believing in kids?

Yes.

We learned all these coveted skills and concepts in a seamless way. In a broad and reductive sense, we learned raw thinking skills—how to solve problems, how to ask hard critical questions—but we also moved beyond the logical mind, to explore ourselves, our relationships, and our experiences in a proactive manner.

### Eye-to-Eye as Activism

Beyond the issue of our personal learning environment, this book has explored the problems we faced as alternative thinkers in a system of education that cannot understand differences as anything other than defects. The roots of this problem run deep, but two obvious ones come to mind. First, many teachers are not educated appropriately about LD/ADHD issues and alternative learning styles; our teachers just do not know any other way to think about us other than as defective.

Second, our schools are ill equipped to provide individualized education on any systematic level. Because of funding pressures within public schools, LD/ADHD children face the developing trend of inclusion—being placed in mainstreamed classrooms to face a hostile educational environment in which only 10 percent of America's teachers are appropriately trained to meet their specialized needs. There are too many kids, too few teachers, and not enough resources to alter the presentation of information to embrace all types of learners adequately. As a result, kids like us grow up feeling all alone and inherently defective.

Although the vast majority of these children are of above-average intelligence, their futures are bleak, and their struggles have broad social consequences for the larger society. More than 50 percent of these children will drop out of high school, abuse substances, or spend time in juvenile hall. As adults, 42 percent of LD/ADHD parents are below or near the federal poverty line, compared to the national average of 16 percent. LD/ADHD adults constitute over 60 percent of adults in literacy programs, 25 to 40 percent of adults on Temporary Assistance for Needy Families (TANEF, formerly AFDC), and 25 to 40 percent of all welfare recipients.

The fundamental mission and premise of Eye-to-Eye has allowed us to play an affirmative role in solving what is in essence our own problem. As successful individuals with LD/ADHD, we work to solve these problems simultaneously on two levels. First, Eye-to-Eye sends LD/ADHD kids a powerful message that they are not defective, they are not alone, and they can be successful. Through early intervention and long-term continuing support, we hope to empower our kids at an early age to take control of their education, hopefully foreclosing the horrific consequences explored in this book.

Second, as successful LD/ADHD individuals in our schools, we force the schools to think differently about kids like us. We ask them to think differently by representing models of LD/ADHD thinkers who have lived beyond the common pathology and proved it a myth. Simultaneously, we provide schools with the extra resources, free of cost, that are necessary to provide a form of individualized education for our Eye-to-Eye kids, and to create an alternative educational environment after school through art. These models of success empower kids like us at a young age and directly challenge the pathological notion that LD/ADHD students are inherently defective.

### Eye-to-Eye as Closure

Project Eye-to-Eye is about empowerment. In the act of service, the act of doing, we are living from a place of fullness, power, and competency. By challenging ourselves and empowering our kids, we have lived beyond the deficit model in our lives, in our schools, and in our institutions of higher education.

Do you remember who we are? We are a kid who did not read until he was twelve and a high school dropout. We made it to an Ivy League school. We beat the system by thinking differently. We moved beyond beating the system by being different. We lived our own theories and proved the experts wrong by giving it all back. We wrote this book.

And now, think fund raising!

# Bibliography

Archambault, Reginald D., ed. *John Dewey on Education: Selected Writings.* Chicago: University of Chicago Press, 1964.

Ellis, Dave. *Becoming a Master Student.* 8th ed. Boston: Houghton Mifflin, 1997.

Gardner, Howard. *The Disciplined Mind: What All Students Should Understand.* New York: Simon & Schuster, 1999.

———. *Frames of Mind: The Theory of Multiple Intelligences.* New York: Basic Books, 1983.

———. *Intelligence Reframed: Multiple Intelligences for the 21st Century.* New York: Basic Books, 1999.

———. *Multiple Intelligences: The Theory in Practice—A Reader.* New York: Basic Books, 1993.

Gilbert, Helen W. *Pathways: A Guide to Reading and Study Skills.* Boston: Houghton Mifflin, 1982.

Greene, Maxine. *Releasing the Imagination: Essays on Education, the Arts and Social Change.* San Francisco: Jossey-Bass, 1995.

Hallowell, Edward M. *Driven to Distraction: Recognizing and Coping with Attention Deficit Disorder from Childhood Through Adulthood.* New York: Simon & Schuster, 1995.

hooks, bell. *Teaching to Transgress: Education as the Practice of Freedom.* New York: Routledge, 1994.

Kraus, Robert. *Leo the Late Bloomer.* New York: Windmill Books, 1971.

Mack, Karin, and Eric Skjei. *Overcoming Writing Blocks.* Los Angeles: Tarcher, 1979.

McWhorter, Kathleen T. *College Reading and Study Skills.* 7th ed. New York: Longman, 1998.

————. *Study and Critical Thinking Skills in College.* 2nd ed. New York: HarperCollins, 1972.

Murphy, Kevin R., and Suzanne LeVert. *Out of the Fog: Treatment Options and Coping Strategies for Adult Attention Deficit Disorder.* New York: Skylight Press, 1995.

Olivier, Carolyn, and Rosemary F. Bowler. *Learning to Learn.* New York: Simon & Schuster, 1996.

Paulk, Walter. *How to* Study *in College.* 4th ed. Boston: Houghton Mifflin, 1989.

Sorenson, Sharon. *How to Write Research Papers.* New York: Macmillan, 1998.

West, Thomas G. *In the Mind's Eye: Visual Thinkers, Gifted People with Learning Difficulties, Computer Images, and the Ironies of Creativity.* Buffalo: Prometheus Books, 1991.

# Index